THE BEGINNER'S GUIDE TO
FLYING ELECTRIC-POWERED AIRPLANES

Other Books in the Doug Pratt's Modeling Guides Series

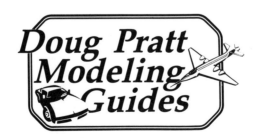

THE BEGINNER'S GUIDE TO
FLYING ELECTRIC-POWERED AIRPLANES

DOUGLAS R. PRATT

TAB | **TAB BOOKS**
Blue Ridge Summit, PA

FIRST EDITION
FIRST PRINTING

Copyright © 1990 by **TAB BOOKS**
Printed in the United States of America

Library of Congress Cataloging-in-Publication Data

Pratt, Douglas R.
   The beginner's guide to flying electric-powered airplanes / by
Douglas R. Pratt.
     p. cm.
   ISBN 0-8306-8451-4
   1. Airplanes—Models—Electric motors. I. Title.
TL777.P72 1990
629.133′1—dc20   89-77307
                                CIP

TAB BOOKS offers software for sale. For information and a catalog, please contact TAB Software Department, Blue Ridge Summit, PA 17294-0850.

Questions regarding the content of this book
should be addressed to:

   Reader Inquiry Branch
   TAB BOOKS
   Blue Ridge Summit, PA 17294-0214

Acquisitions Editor: Jeff Worsinger
Book Editor: Steven H. Mesner
Production: Katherine Brown

Contents

Introduction

THIS BOOK IS WRITTEN FOR PEOPLE who have decided to try building and flying radio controlled airplanes, and are considering an electric-powered plane for their first attempt. Experienced gas-powered model fliers will also find this information helpful when they consider trying electric flight.

Why electric power? Electric-powered RC flying is more than just a curiosity; it's a category with distinctive pluses and minuses. On the minus side, electric power systems don't have as good a power-to-weight ratio as gas models, since a glow engine and its fuel tank are almost always lighter than an electric motor and battery pack of equivalent power. Flight times are somewhat limited; 10 minutes is a good flight for an electric job, while a gas model can carry a big fuel tank and fly for half an hour. And of course, it takes 15 or 20 minutes to recharge an electric flight battery pack—much less time than it takes to refill a fuel tank!

On the other hand, electric flight has many charms. You'll never have trouble starting the motor, and there's no carburetor to adjust. Electric power systems are reliable and simple. They make very little noise. And you don't have to wipe exhaust off your airplane at the end of the day.

Electrics have a strong attraction for beginning RC fliers. This is especially true for folks who have been running RC cars. They have an advantage, because they've already learned how to charge batteries and handle electric motors. In fact, they have a lot of the equipment they'll need already.

The first three chapters of this book will give you basic information that applies generally to electric-powered RC models. Then we'll look at sixteen popular electric RC airplanes in depth. If you're considering buying one of these models, you should find good information on it here—but you should look over the other kit reviews as well.

I selected kits that would represent the different types of electric models you can buy: kits and ready-builts, sailplanes and conventional planes, old-timers and aerobatic jobs. There's information in each review that applies to similar planes. It was impossible to review every electric plane on the market (I nearly went crazy revising the book to include models that were released after I started writing!), but the planes that are presented here are a good overview of the models you'll be able to buy.

1

Getting Started

GENERALLY SPEAKING, THERE ARE TWO ways to buy model airplane supplies: from a local hobby shop, and from mail-order companies. I recommend buying from a hoppy shop if you can. The reason is simple: *service*. You're going to need help getting your new RC plane into the air and learning how to fly it. Flying RC is like driving a car. You don't just climb in and drive away; you need help learning. A good hobby shop is the best place to get this help.

Your local store will know what you're going through. They can answer your tenderfoot questions without embarrassing you. They have the products that you need *when* you need them. If you get stuck, they're as close as the phone. Ask any loyal customer of a good hobby shop—there's no better way to enjoy the sport of RC.

MODELING BY MAIL

If there's no store near you, or if the local store doesn't carry what you need, you'll have to go the mail-order route. That's why this book lists the names and addresses of several mail-order companies in the Appendix.

Mail-order will get you the products you need, but you'll be short on information. It's hard for a mail-order company to get you what you need to *know*. There are two companies, however, that do a good job of it—and by good luck, they just happen to have a lot of electric models!

Hobby Lobby International in Tennessee imports the excellent Graupner line of electric planes and products from Germany. Their catalog has a wealth of good information for the beginner. Best of all, when you call Hobby Lobby, you can talk to a modeler. I can give them an unqualified recommendation.

Doug's Hobby Shop (no relation—honest!) is really a chain of seven stores, plus a mail-order operation. Because they have so many retail stores, they have many folks handy who know how to help beginners. They also have an excellent stock of electric supplies, as well as good delivery.

The Keystone RC Club in Hatfield, PA, has been holding an Electric Fly-In for over 10 years. Hundreds of modelers from all over the East Coast show up for a great weekend of flying.

Part of the author's fleet of electric airplanes. Since you don't have to carry fuel, starters, and other accessories for electric planes, you can fit more of them in your car!

A cloud of electric airplanes takes to the sky at the Keystone RC Club Electric Fly-In. The last one down wins a cash prize!

MODELNET

Finally, if you have a computer and a modem, you have access to a splendid source of information available to you 24 hours a day. The CompuServe Information Service has a service called ModelNet, run by model fliers. You can access ModelNet to look for clubs and hobby shops in your area, scan calendars for national modeling events, and read newsletter articles from all over the country. Best of all, you can use ModelNet's message board to get your questions answered. With literally hundreds of messages posted every week, it's a rare message that doesn't get a few answers within a day or so. Call CompuServe toll-free at (800) 848-8990 for complete information on how to hook up to the network.

ACADEMY OF MODEL AERONAUTICS

There is a national organization of model fliers called the Academy of Model Aeronautics. Everyone who flies RC model airplanes should be an AMA member.

The strongest reason to join AMA is the fact that your AMA membership covers you with accident and liability insurance. Many flying site owners won't allow you to fly on their land unless you have some form of insurance, so they can't get sued for giving you permission to fly. This is the case at most of the club flying fields in the country. If it were not for AMA insurance, it would be next to impossible to find a place to fly, unless you're lucky enough to live on a farm.

The AMA insurance covers you in several

VOLUME 6 • 1986

There's a quarterly magazine for model fliers published on videotape: *RC Video Magazine*. Each tape covers many different topics, with plenty of material on electric flight.

The Prairie Bird is a wonderful trainer plane from Peck-Polymers. Parts are included in the kit to allow either a small glow engine or a Leisure electric geared system for power. It's a truly gentle flier that's easy to build.

important ways. If you have an accident and are injured by your model plane, and your own health insurance doesn't cover it (or you don't have health insurance), your AMA insurance will. If you cause injury or property damage to someone else, and your homeowner's insurance won't cover it, your AMA insurance will. Worst of all, if you get sued, your AMA insurance will be there to help. In this lawsuit-happy society, this is no small matter.

Model clubs have been hauled into court for making noise!

AMA membership also gets you a subscription to *Model Aviation,* one of the finest model magazines available. You'll have competition privileges at AMA-sanctioned events all over the country. And AMA works for you in other important ways, too. It was AMA's work with the FCC that made it possible to fly radio control without having to get a ham radio license first.

AMA charters over 2500 local clubs in all areas of the country. These clubs will probably be the focal point of your activity in radio control; they are the best way to enjoy RC. Clubs have nice flying fields, where you can fly safely. Most clubs have instructors who will help you learn to fly without using up airplanes in the process. There will certainly be friendly folks at the field who will help you check out your equipment and answer your questions.

Joining an AMA-chartered club is the best way to get started in RC. When you consider the time, effort, and grief you'll save by being hooked up with experienced RC fliers, the club dues are a real bargain. Call or write the AMA for the name and address of a club in your area.

2

Electric Basics

ELECTRIC-POWERED MODEL PLANES are not all that different from other model planes. You use the same skills in building and flying them, as well as the same tools, glues, and materials.

SELECTING AN ELECTRIC PLANE

Thanks to the increasing popularity of electric flight, you've got quite a range of choices when you want to select an electric plane. If you're a beginner, look for a high-wing plane with lightweight construction and a conventional power system that doesn't require more than a six-cell battery pack. If you're already an experienced modeler and are looking for an electric model to compare to the planes you've already flown, you still have a good choice. But you should be prepared to buy an advanced charger that's capable of charging flight packs with as many as 20 cells.

We'll be taking an in-depth look at a lot of electric models in Chapter 4. These models were selected to give a good overview of the kits that are commonly available through hobby stores. You can get a good idea of what it'll take to build and fly just about any electric model from these representative reviews.

KIT OR ARF?

One of the first choices you'll have to make is whether to build your airplane from a kit or buy an ARF (almost-ready-to-fly) plane.

There are several factors to consider. If you build a kit, it'll take longer to get in the air. On the other hand, you'll learn a lot more, and you'll know how to repair the plane if you crash. Most kits fly better than ARFs. Some ARFs use exotic materials (such as laminated foam) for construction that's difficult to fix if it breaks. Most ARFs are imported, and sometimes the instructions are poorly translated. ARFs are *always* more expensive than kits that you build yourself.

On the plus side, there are some ARFs that fly very well. Many are very well-designed and will be ready to fly with one or two evenings of work.

5

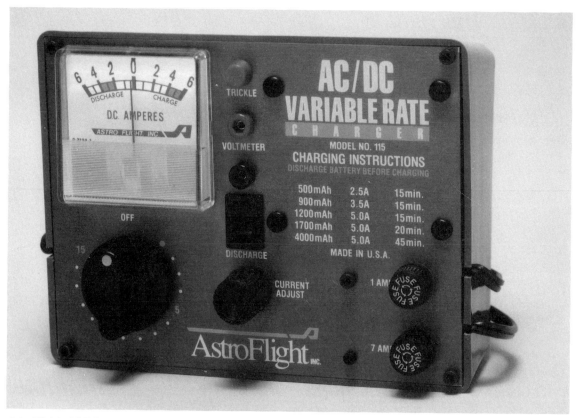

Astro Flight's AC/DC Variable Rate Charger is excellent for packs with up to eight cells. It will charge cells with capacities as low as 500 MAh, and can work from house current.

It's up to you. I often suggest that beginners start with both an ARF and a kit plane. For example, a Futaba Professor will get you in the air fast with a very good-flying plane. And you can take your time building a kit plane for your second model. By the time you've torn up the first plane with the inevitable mistakes, the second plane will be ready to go.

CONVERTING KITS TO ELECTRIC FLIGHT

You also have the option of converting just about any gas-powered model to electric flight. My buddy Dave Peltz took some time out from his fancy sailplanes a few years ago and built a SIG Quarter Scale Piper Cub. He installed an Astro Flight Cobalt motor system, and made no effort at all to lighten the structure or adapt it for electric power except

for the box he built on the firewall to fit the engine. It flies beautifully, and still does everything the Cub could do with a gas engine—for about five minutes.

The point that Dave proved is that you don't *have* to make major changes to a conventional airplane to use electric power on it. Of course, you will get longer flight times and better performance from planes that are relatively light and have light wing loading (relatively large wings for their weight). So if you want to electrify a gas-powered model, look for a light plane with a big wing.

Just about any sailplane kit can be converted to electric flight. Carl Goldberg Models sells a power pod for their popular Sophisticated Lady sailplane that works well on other sailplane designs, too. Look for a model with a fuselage that's wide enough to take your battery pack without much crowding. The battery, which is the heaviest part of

The Twin Rapid Charger is sold by Hobby Lobby International. It'll charge two battery packs at once from the 12 volt battery in your car—great way to keep flying!

Astro's DC/DC Constant Amp Charger can charge packs with up to 20 cells. This is the charger you need for large motor systems such as the Cobalt 40.

the electric power system, should go as near as possible to the plane's center of gravity. This is usually right underneath the wing.

Mike Green has been very successful with a SIG Riser 100 that he converted to electric power. He sent me this note on ModelNet after his first few test flights:

"My goal was to make a large electric glider with a wing loading comparable to a standard glider. By bringing it in at 50 ounces, I am able to power it with the same 05-geared Astro Flight system that I use on the Challenger 2 meter glider. This plane will glide forever! It behaves like an unpowered glider in the glide and the power from this motor system is ample. The rate of climb is only slightly less than on the Challenger, which is a smaller plane.

"I made a few changes to make the Riser 100 lighter; I don't believe I've sacrificed too much strength. I substituted hard balsa $5/8$-inch square sticks for the hardwood leading edges, dispensed with the $1/4$-inch steel rod wing joiner and made it solid here with a plywood brace, and made detachable wingtips (with the Ace RC wing joiners). That steel rod is to make the wing strong enough to withstand a winch launch, and electric flight is a lot gentler. I slide battery packs in from the front top hatch. It's really a great flier!"

Another gas-powered model that's ripe for electric conversion is the SIG Kadet Seniorita. This big, light airplane is designed to use .20 to .25 size gas motors. In my experience, a K&B .20 Sportster engine is almost more power than a Seniorita needs. I'm certain that an Astro Flight Cobalt 15 system would fly the Seniorita just as well as the K&B .20 gas motor. In fact, the Seniorita would probably do just fine with a Leisure geared 05 on seven cells.

BATTERY SELECTION

Most electric flight systems will use battery packs of either six or seven cells. The larger systems, such as the Astro Flight 15, 40, and 60 systems, will require larger packs. These are not very common; only one of the planes we talk about later in this book uses a battery pack of more than seven cells.

You can get by very nicely with battery packs designed for RC cars. These are made up of cells of 1200 milliamp-hour (MAh) capacity. They're sometimes called "sub-C" cells, which refers to the size of the cell. You will find six-cell 1200 MAh cell packs are inexpensive and readily available at hobby shops.

Sometimes you will find that you have a choice of cell brands. My own experience is that Sanyo cells are the best in terms of consistency and durability.

Whenever you can, I recommend using seven-cell packs. The weight of the extra cell doesn't affect performance that much, and the extra voltage the cell provides will dramatically improve the power. This gives you a better climb and gets you upstairs faster, letting you reach that comfortable "two mistakes high" altitude in a hurry. I've gotten to the point where I use seven-cell packs in almost everything I fly.

If weight is a problem, you can use smaller cells in the pack. 800 MAh cells are only a little larger than the AA cells in your transmitter and receiver, and are much lighter than 1200 MAh cells. A seven-cell pack of 800 MAh cells weighs a little less than a six-cell pack of 1200 MAh cells! In light planes, you get the extra punch of seven cells without the weight. 800 MAh cell packs are also very useful in planes with slim fuselages, where there isn't enough room to cram in the larger cells.

The battery packs made and sold by SR Batteries deserve special attention. These packs are more expensive than just about any other packs that you can buy, but what you get for your money is more power for the weight. The cells in a sub-C size SR pack have a capacity of 1800 MAh instead of the usual 1200 MAh. If you need the smaller, lighter cells, SR makes packs of cells that are the same size as the 800 MAh cells from other manufacturers, but they're rated at 1200 MAh. All SR packs are charged, cycled, and tested at the factory. In my experience, they are well worth the extra cost.

CHARGING

There are two important ways to charge a battery pack: fast and slow. *Fast-charging* is what you want to do on the field, so you can get back in the air. However, if you overcharge while fast-charging, you'll heat up the pack. Heat is the enemy of battery packs—get them too warm and the vents will open in the cells, allowing the expanding chemicals inside the cells to escape. This is better than having a cell burst, but it will quickly reduce capacity and ruin the cell.

Slow-charging takes from eight to 16 hours. The advantage of slow-charging is that it doesn't warm the cells. It also performs the very important job of "balancing" the battery pack. You see, each cell accepts a charge at a slightly different rate from the other cells it's connected to. This means that all the cells in the pack don't achieve full charge at the same time, so some cells will be fully charged while others are still charging. Since a fully charged cell converts the charge current into heat, these cells are in danger. If you're fast-charging, you can actually vent one or two cells before the others are completely charged!

The way to avoid this is to "balance" the pack. Slow-charging brings all the cells up to peak charge over a longer period of time. The low current going through the pack won't heat up the fully-charged cells while the other cells are catching up. A pack that has been slow-charged and discharged ("cycled") several times will be in a balanced condition, in which the cells all accept a charge at close to the same rate.

All you really have to do to keep your packs balanced is to slow-charge them the night before you go flying, the same as the batteries in your transmitter and receiver. You'll begin to notice that the first flight of the day always gets the longest battery run! This is because the slow charge is putting a 100 percent charge into each cell of your battery pack. After a typical day of six or even flights (with fast-charges in between), take your pack home and slow-charge it again. Slow-charging is the way to keep your packs healthy.

CHARGERS

Selecting a charger is very important. Thanks to RC cars, there are some very inexpensive chargers available. RC car technology has also given us electric fliers the benefit of some great battery charging technology.

If you're on a tight budget, the under-$50 chargers will charge a typical six- or seven-cell 1200 MAh battery pack adequately. Be sure that the charger you buy has a "trickle charge" circuit to allow you to slow-charge the batteries. You'll have to power these chargers with a 12-volt auto battery. Since these chargers are only controlled by a timer, make sure you don't overheat the packs by fast-charging them too much.

I have a simple charger from Hobby Lobby that I use a lot. The most useful thing about this Twin Rapid Charger is that it will fast-charge *two* battery packs at once. This is a great way to keep flying all day!

Spending a little more money gets you a charger that works with house current. The convenience is well worth it.

The best chargers to have are the *peak detectors*. These automatically detect when the battery is fully charged and switch from fast-charging to slow-charging. This prevents overcharging and heating of the cells. It also assures you of getting close to a 100 percent charge each time you use the charger, without risking your packs.

You'll pay more for a peak detector charger, so you might as well get the most versatile charger you can. Look for a charger with a variable charge rate. The variable rate will allow you to charge packs with different size cells. One of my favorite chargers is the Novak Peak Plus. By varying the charge current, I can charge almost any battery with it, even the batteries in my transmitters and receivers.

Cougar Mountain Products has recently introduced a neat new product called the Pro Auto Peak. This is a little box that plugs into the battery connector on your charger. You plug your battery into the Pro Auto peak, turn the charger on to fast-charge, and push the button on the box. The Pro

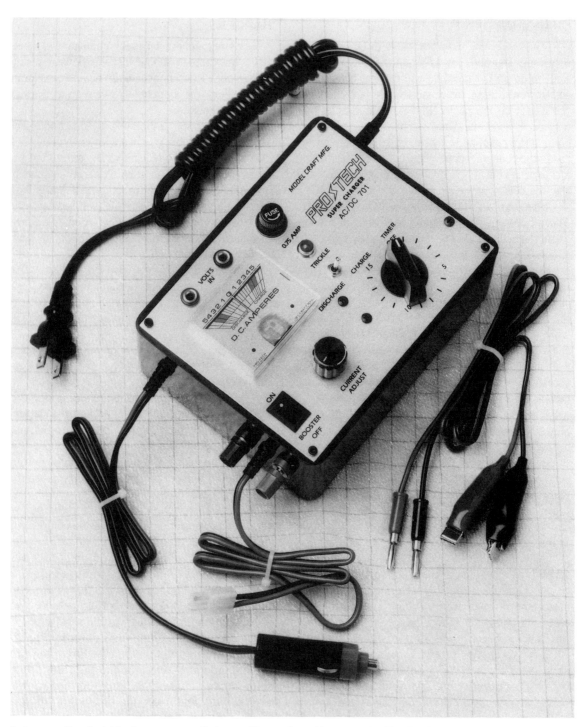

A charger with adjustable charge current will charge different sizes of battery packs. This Pro-Tech unit can charge up to seven cell packs, with cell sizes from 500 MAh to 1200 MAh.

Auto Peak will detect a full charge and shut off the current to the pack. This inexpensive little gizmo lets you turn any charger into a peak detector.

MOTORS

When you're just starting out, you don't really have to know a lot about electric motors. Many trainer kits come with motors, and some ARFs come with the motors already installed.

There are two basic types of electric motors that we use in planes, distinguished by the material used in the motor magnets. The vast majority of motors use *ferrite* magnets. These are inexpensive and adequate for most uses. Motors with *samarium cobalt* magnets have considerably more power than ferrite motors. They're also more expensive, and they use up a battery pack faster. Cobalt motors are often the best choice for heavier or higher-performance airplanes.

Motor drive systems also fall into two groups. Most electric planes use direct-drive systems, in which the propeller is mounted right on the shaft of the electric motor. Since electric motors perform best at high rpm, smaller props are used to take advantage of this. However, in many applications, a larger prop will provide more thrust. Electric power systems can be made to swing larger props by using a gear-down setup, converting the high-speed output of the electric motor to turn a high-torque larger prop.

You should always use the electric motor and drive system recommended by the kit manufacturer. They've tested it and they know that it works. If you want to experiment, you should at least start with the recommended motor.

CONNECTORS

The connectors used to connect the drive battery pack to the electric power system in the airplane are important. If you use the wrong connector, or one that's old or corroded, it can soak up a lot of the power that should be flying your airplane. I've had a bad connector get so hot in flight that it turned into a fuse and broke apart.

Most electric power systems come with *Tamiya* connectors. This name comes from the common brand of RC cars. These connectors have white plastic bodies and clips that hold the male and female connectors together. These connectors are simple and reliable, and more than adequate for most uses. However, they can corrode. Inspect the contacts every now and then. If you see black or greenish corrosion on the contact, cut off the connector and replace it.

Sermos connectors are very popular with electric fliers. These connectors have less internal resistance than other common brands, and their contacts are easier to clean. They're rather bulky, and can be hard to assemble without special tools. I use them in most of my electric planes.

The Miniblitz is an inexpensive speed controller from Hobby Lobby. I used it in the Goldberg Mirage. It comes with a safety switch that mounts outside the fuselage.

SWITCHES AND SPEED CONTROLLERS

Your power system will need some way of turning the motor on and off while the plane's in the air. This can range from a simple on-off switch hooked to a servo, to an electronic device that allows you to control the speed of the motor with the throttle stick.

Most of the electric kits we've looked at in this book recommend a switch; many even come with the switch already wired in. These work just fine and are nice and simple. However, you'll almost always get better performance if you use a proportional speed controller.

A speed controller plugs into the throttle channel of your receiver. It varies the speed of the motor depending on the position of the throttle stick. This allows you to find a "cruise" speed for maximum battery life (we discuss this more in the airplane kit reviews). It also makes it easier to turn geared motor systems on and off; gradually applying power to the gears is much less likely to break them than suddenly switching on full power.

There are many different brands of speed controllers. Most are designed for RC cars, but will work just fine in electric-powered airplanes. Look for controllers that are small and lightweight. The controller should have an adjustment that will let you set the *high point* (the point at which the motor is getting full power from the battery pack). Read the instructions carefully and set the controller up the way it tells you to.

Many car speed controllers come with a

JoMar makes a wide range of speed controllers and on-off switches that have become the industry standard. The newer models use tiny surface-mount components.

Futaba's Attack 4NBL radio system is designed specifically for electric flight. The receiver incorporates a proportional speed controller, battery eliminator circuit, and voltage sensor in one package.

"BEC" feature. This stands for *battery eliminator circuit,* and means that the speed controller will supply power to the receiver from the drive battery. This makes it unnecessary to carry a separate battery for the receiver in the car. I don't recommend that you do this in a plane! If you fly long enough to run down the drive battery, it will drop below the voltage needed to run the receiver, and you'll lose

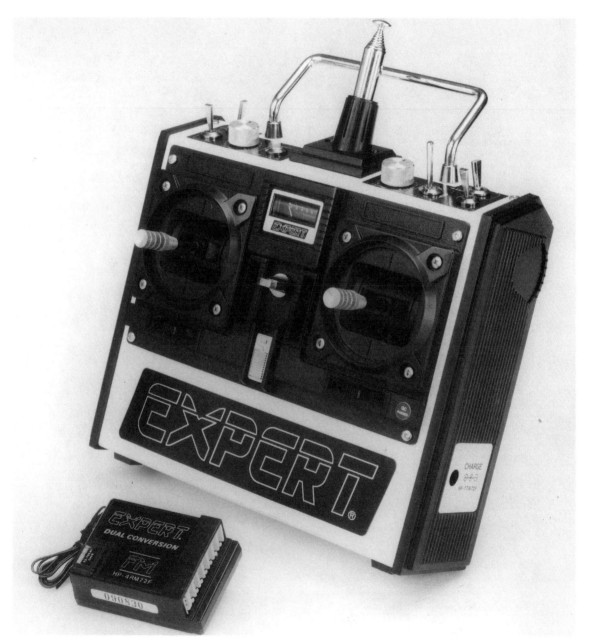

World Engines imports the Expert series RC systems. The new FM Expert is an excellent radio. Micro servos are available.

control of the airplane. Use a separate battery for the receiver. Your receiver battery can be very small, since it will only be used when the drive battery is low. I have several planes with this kind of speed controller, and I use small 100 MAh receiver packs from Ace RC and SR Batteries.

RADIO SYSTEMS

Generally speaking, any radio system with a lightweight receiver, small servos, and a small battery pack is just fine for electric planes. Since most electric planes don't fly at high speeds, large, powerful servos are unnecessary.

I have had very good success with several common radio systems, and can recommend them for your use. Airtronics makes fine radios, and their receivers and servos are very small and light. Ace RC's Olympic 5 radio is excellent for electrics; it comes without servos, so you only have to buy as many as you need. Futaba's inexpensive Attack series radios are available with mini receivers and servos, and are very good for electrics. The Max series radios from JR are also very good for electrics; they can be bought with mini servos. The Cox Cadet III single-stick three-channel system is very small and light, and works great in electric models.

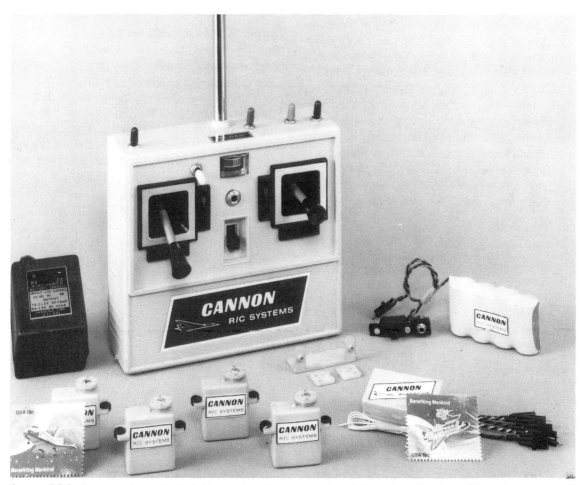

Cannon RC Systems are absolutely the lightest and smallest you can buy. A three-channel system, with receiver, servos and battery, weighs less than three ounces!

SPECIALIZED RADIOS

There are three radio systems I've used in Electric models that deserve some special attention. The first is the in Futaba Attack MCR-4A system. This inexpensive four-channel RC set was designed specifically for electric flight. The transmitter features servo reversing switches and a comfortable hand-grip design. It comes with two micro-sized servos.

The important part of the MCR-4A system is the receiver. This receiver incorporates an electronic speed controller, a battery eliminator circuit, and a voltage sensing cutoff circuit into one package.

Installing this system in your plane allows you to have complete proportional control of the motor speed with the throttle stick. It doesn't need a separate battery pack to power the receiver; the receiver takes the power that it needs from the drive battery. When the drive battery starts to run down, the voltage sensing circuit shuts the motor off. It's set so that there's plenty of power to run the receiver after the motor is shut off, so you can stay up and thermal around as long as you want.

In my opinion, this is one of the best ways to fly electrics. I have three of these radios, and have been very pleased with the performance.

The second special system isn't an RC system at all. It's the Graupner Power Switch, sold by Hobby Lobby. The Power Switch is designed to work with JR radios, but can be adapted to other brands by changing the receiver plug.

The Power Switch gives you the ability to turn the motor on and off with the transmitter stick. It also incorporates a battery eliminator circuit and a voltage detector. This functions the same way as the Futaba MCR-4A receiver: It shuts off the motor when the battery gets low. I have had very good results with this system. (See my discussion of the Graupner Elektro-UHU sailplane in Chapter 4 for details of my tests with this system.)

The third special radio system isn't specifically for electrics, but it's remarkable because it's the lightest RC system available. Cannon RC Systems is a small company that's known worldwide for their pioneering work in micro-miniature RC systems. Their radios are all handmade, and are not inexpensive. They are available in hobby shops, but not may stores carry them, so you'll probably have to order a system direct from Cannon. But in an installation where light weight is crucial, there's nothing better. A Cannon flight system, with a receiver, battery pack, and three servos, weighs only 2 $3/4$ ounces!

3

First Flights

RADIO CONTROL FLYING, LIKE BASEBALL and some other activities, is largely a mental exercise. Your preparation, your attitude, and your ability to think through stressful situations are important to your success and enjoyment.

TWO IMPORTANT RULES

I've distilled a lot of the good advice I've gotten over the years into two simple rules for beginners to keep in mind. These two thoughts will get you through most of the "panic" situations that low-time pilots encounter.

Rule 1 is: *The plane knows how to fly better than you do*. Trainer planes are designed to be stable and self-correcting. This means that if you get your plane into a bad situation (usually spiraling straight at the ground, while you frantically try to remember which way to turn), releasing the sticks will allow the plane to straighten itself out. This might sound hard to believe, but it's true! Aerodynamic forces will bring the plane out of the turn; it will still be coming down, but once you stop spiraling, you can

pull the elevator stick back and get back upstairs where you belong. This is why most instructors will tell you to immediately climb up to a good altitude to give the plane time to recover—an altitude commonly known as "two mistakes high," meaning that you can make *two* mistakes before hitting the ground.

What if you're too low to give the plane a chance to straighten itself out? Releasing the stick is *still* the best thing you can do. If the plane hits the ground in a tight turn, you will probably tear the wing off the fuselage and damage the tail. If the plane has had a chance to straighten itself out before it hits, it should hit on the lower nose section of the fuselage, which is generally one of the stronger parts of its structure. In a crash, much of the damage will be done by the heavy battery pack moving forward. If the plane is leveling out when it hits, the pack will have less forward momentum.

In any case, you can count on your plane's ability to fly itself out of most situations—provided, of course, that it's trimmed properly. Trimming is one

John Worth, AMA's retired Executive Director, gets ready to launch Bill Winter's Heron high-performance electric design. Winter is at the controls. The Heron is now a kit from Davey Systems.

of the best reasons to let an experienced pilot fly your plane first. We'll discuss trimming in more detail a little later.

Rule 2 is intended to help in the situation where the beginner has the most problems: when the plane is coming straight at him. Think about it. When the plane is flying away from you and you move the rudder stick to the left, the plane banks to your left. But when it's coming *at* you, and you move the stick to the left, the plane banks to your *right*! It's going to take some experience to overcome the feeling of disorientation you'll get when this happens. One common method of dealing with this is the ''over the shoulder'' technique, where

you continually turn so that you and the plane are facing in the same direction, even though this usually means you're looking back over your shoulder at the airplane. I prefer to get comfortable when I'm flying (sometimes I fly from a lawn chair), so this kind of body English really doesn't appeal to me. I prefer Rule 2, which states: *When the plane is coming toward you, level the wings by moving the stick toward the low wing.*

Visualize this situation: Your plane is on final approach, lined up with the runway and coming at you in a glide. One wing starts to drop. You move your stick toward the side where the low wing is to bring it back up. In other words, if the left wing (as

Keith Shaw's masterful aerobatic biplane flies with an Astro 40 Cobalt motor system, and even has smoke!

viewed from the plane) starts to drop, you move the stick to your right. Try it—it works! Eventually this will become reflex, and you won't have to keep reminding yourself.

WHERE TO FLY

The very best place to fly radio control models is on an AMA club field. The clubs have the best fields, with nice runways, good pit areas, and friendly club members to help you out. They will also have safety rules in place, so you can be sure that you can fly safely at their field.

It's easy to find a club in your area. The first place to look is your local hobby shop. If you don't have a store near you, write or call the AMA. They will refer you to one of their over 2500 clubs around the nation. AMA's address and phone number are in the Appendix at the back of this book.

If there's no club near you, you can fly electric planes from any open field, such as a park or athletic field. However, there are some rules that you must follow when flying at such a site. First and foremost, contact the owner of the land and *get permission* to fly there. Don't assume that since it's a public park you can fly on it whenever you please. Second, make sure that there's enough unobstructed area to fly your plane safely. You want to spend your time flying, not threading your way through trees, goalposts, and electric wires. *You must not fly your model over people at any time.*

Never fly near electric wires; they can generate interference.

SAFETY RULES

As with any activity, there are safety rules that must be obeyed. To ignore them is to put yourself, your plane, and any spectators at an unnecessary risk.

If you fly at a club field (by far the best way to fly), read and understand their safety rules. All AMA-chartered clubs start with the basic AMA Safety Code for their rules, then add rules that handle specific situations for their field. Violating these safety rules can jeopardize your insurance coverage, and your fellow club members won't appreciate it either.

Electric planes aren't subject to some of the safety rules needed for gas-powered planes.

There's no flammable fuel, for example. But there are important rules for electrics that should always be followed. Here's a quick rundown.

1. Use a motor switch. There should always be a separate switch on the outside of the plane that turns the motor on and off. This keeps the motor from starting up until you're ready for it. You might think that the radio-operated switch or speed controller is enough, but what if the receiver gets switched on accidentally? Interference from another radio on the same frequency could start your motor at a very bad time.

2. Turn your transmitter on first, then your receiver. If your receiver goes on first, and your motor switch is left on, your motor could start up at the wrong time and surprise you. Many speed controllers are designed so that they default to the "off" position if there's no signal from a transmit-

More of Keith Shaw's amazing electric jobs. The big Gee Bee R-1 flies with an Astro Flight Cobalt 40 motor, and is fully aerobatic.

ter, but strong interference might fool the controller into switching on.

3. Respect the motor! Be sure the transmitter and receiver are *on* and the motor switch is *off* before you plug in the drive battery. Switch on the motor just before launch. Think about it: When you stick your finger into a prop driven by a gas motor, it stops the motor. But an electric motor tries to keep turning.

4. Respect the other fliers. Make sure they know you're flying an electric model. If you need to go onto the runway for a hand launch, make sure the other pilots know that you're going out there, and tell them when you're done. *Don't* count on them to see what you're doing; they're concentrating on their own planes.

5. Never fly over people's heads! Stay in the areas designated for flying. Avoid the pits. Most of all, avoid flying over your own head; this can disorient you quickly.

PREFLIGHT CHECKLIST

Just as pilots of full-scale airplanes go through a preflight checklist before they take off, there are certain checks you should always make.

1. Is the radio system charged? If this is your first flight of the day, and you charged your transmitter and receiver overnight the night before, you're ready. If this is your third or fourth flight of the day, you should check your receiver batteries.

There are several battery meters available for this purpose. My favorite is the Ace RC Voltmaster, which gives you a meter reading of the receiver pack voltage with or without a load.

2. Is the drive battery pack fully charged? See our discussion of chargers and charging in Chapter 2.

3. Walkaround. This check is just like the ones full-scale pilots do. Look all over the plane. Is the prop tight? Have any of the wing rubber bands slipped? Are the clevises on the rudder and elevator horns snapped tightly? Are the wheel collars tight? Is the landing gear straight? Are the tail surfaces still straight and firmly attached?

4. Radio check. After you have clearance to use the frequency, turn on your transmitter, then your receiver. Leave the motor switch off. Wiggle all controls and make sure they're moving in the correct directions: back stick for up elevator, left stick for left rudder, etc. Now collapse the antenna of the transmitter fully, place the plane on the ground, and start walking away. You should be able to get at least 30 paces away and still have control, even with the antenna down.

If your radio system doesn't pass the range test, don't fly! There's something wrong somewhere. It might be that your receiver pack needs charging. Or there might be something more serious happening, such as a loose connection or a cracked crystal. Sending in your radio for service when it consistently fails a range test is a smart move; it's a lot cheaper than tearing up an airplane.

LAUNCHING

Okay, you're ready to go. Check the sky one more time to see who else is in the air. Remember, anyone who is setting up an approach to land has the right of way; wait for them to complete their landing. If you're not flying on a club field, make sure *you* know where everyone is, and make sure *they* know that you're flying. Make certain that you have plenty of overfly area, that you won't be flying over people at any time, and that people won't wander out in the area you'll need to land on.

There are three ways to launch: Have a friend hand-launch your plane, hand-launch it yourself, or take off from the ground. Ground takeoffs are easy if done from a hard dirt or paved runway, but will use more battery power than hand-launches. Having a friend launch for you is best for your first flights, because you can concentrate on flying.

All your friend has to do is get the plane up to flying speed and launch it straight. This will take a few running steps. Electric planes have more than enough power to rise out of your hand. Have your launcher hold the plane pointing straight ahead, with the wings level. This is the same way it should be launched. Don't let him do a javelin throw with the nose in the air. In fact, don't let him throw it at all! Tell him to just hold it straight, take a few running steps, and let it fly itself right out of his hand.

When you're ready to launch it yourself, you should keep the same thing in mind. Hold the plane in your right hand (or, if you're left-handed, your left hand), with your fingers at the center of gravity. Get a comfortable grip—not so that you can *throw* the plane, but so that you can control it and keep it straight and level as you move.

Hold the transmitter in your left hand. When you're ready to launch, you can use your left thumb to move the throttle stick up. Take a few steps and feel the plane rise out of your hand. When it does, move the transmitter into your right hand, and walk back to the pilot's area.

It's easier than it sounds. Keep your motions smooth and relaxed, and you won't make it harder than it has to be.

Taking off from the ground is even simpler. Point the plane into the wind, advance the throttle, and use the rudder to keep the plane running straight down the runway. It should lift off by itself as soon as it reaches flying speed. A little bit of up elevator may be necessary to get it unstuck from the runway.

IN THE AIR

Don't try to climb out too steeply. You may use too much up elevator, which will slow the plane.

The author launches his electric-powered Prairie Bird. With the engine almost idling, this plane will give you slow, beautiful 15-minute flights.

Most electric models (especially trainers) are designed so that you can't stall them by putting in so much up that you slow them beyond flying speed. Still, it's unnerving to be clawing for altitude and have one wingtip drop suddenly because the plane is at stall speed. You have to have presence of mind enough to let the nose come down so the plane can pick up speed again.

TRIMMING

Once you're in the air, you can trim the plane so that it flies smoothly. The idea is to use the small slide switches under and to the left of the stick to set the control surface positions so that the plane flies straight and level when the stick is centered. Are you holding the stick back to keep the nose from dropping? Pull the elevator trim (to the left of the stick) back until the nose stays level. Does the plane try to turn to the right all by itself? Move the rudder trim (under the stick) to the left until the wings stay level.

Sometimes you find that you have to move the trim switch all the way one way or the other. Maybe that still isn't enough to keep the plane level. In such a case, land as soon as you can and adjust the pushrods.

Suppose you have to add full right trim to keep the plane flying straight. When the plane is on the ground, move the rudder trim back to the center. Remove the clevis from the rudder horn, and screw it in or out so that the rudder will be held slightly to the right when it's reattached. If the elevator required a lot of trim, change the elevator clevis the same way.

If you find that the plane needs a lot of rudder trim, this could indicate a warped wing. See the discussion in Chapter 4 of the Polk Juicer kit for instructions on how to check and correct a wing warp.

TURNS

Model airplanes spend most of their time turning. It's important to develop your turning skills so that you can point the plane where you want and keep it there.

The first thing to learn about turning is that it's done with the elevator, not the rudder or ailerons. Rudder and ailerons *bank* the plane, they don't turn it. It's the elevator that makes the turn happen and controls how fast it is.

Let's go through a typical turn to the left. First, you add left rudder. This banks the plane, rolling it so that the right wing points up and the left wing points down. Most planes will not require much rudder to stay in the bank, but you'll have to hold slight left pressure on the stick to keep the plane from rolling back to level flight. Once the plane is at about a 45-degree angle, pull the stick back. This adds up elevator, pulling the plane through the turn. Watch the plane and control the elevator so that the nose remains level. The nose will tend to drop after you have banked the plane; simply add enough up to keep the nose level, and it will pull smoothly through the turn.

As the plane turns around and comes closer to traveling in the direction that you want, start to feed in right rudder. This will level the plane and allow it to fly straight. As the left wing moves back up you'll feel the nose of the plane beginning to rise; release the up elevator you've been holding, and let the nose stay level. Soon you're straight and level on your new heading.

As you practice, you'll learn when to start leveling the wings by applying opposite rudder, and when to release the up elevator. Your turns will smooth out as you do. Making wide, lazy figure-eights is a good way to practice turning. When you can turn the plane so that it always travels through the center of your imaginary figure eight, you've mastered the art of turning.

LANDING

Now for the most important part of your flying skills—landing! As an old friend of mine once said, "Takeoffs are optional; landings are mandatory!"

For your first few flights, you should start practicing your landings before your drive batteries quit. This gives you enough juice to decide that you don't like the approach, fire the motor back up, and get back upstairs to set up another landing.

Jim Martin of Hobby Lobby shows off the amazing Graupner Race Rat at the KRC Electric Fly-In. This plane can keep up with a gas-powered racer!

If you get into a situation where you have to land, remember a rule that full-scale pilots use in similar situations: Pretend there's a runway underneath you, and land on it. Don't try to make low-altitude turns to get the plane lined up on the runway. Just try to miss major obstructions, and bring it in as smoothly as you can. You'll minimize any damage that way.

With most trainer planes, your approach will start in a power-off glide. Turn the plane so that it's lined up with the runway, and let it settle down to the ground, concentrating on keeping the wings level.

This is where our "Point the stick at the low wing" rule comes in very handy! The plane's coming at you, and the left wing starts to drop. That's the wing on the far side—your right. Move the stick toward that wing and it comes back up.

Give the plane time to come down. If you overshoot the runway you are unlikely to damage the plane. You should resist the temptation to abort the landing and go around, unless you're no longer lined up with the runway or there's some obstruction ahead. After all, if your battery has just barely enough power left to stagger back into the air, it's unlikely that you'll be able to get back to the other end of the runway, and you'll probably have to put the plane down in a worse place.

Once you're down, the first thing to do is to go over to the plane and switch off the motor. Then get yourself and the plane off the runway to clear the way for other pilots who might need to land.

Practice, practice, practice! The more you fly, the more natural it will all become. Practice is the best way to perfect your flying technique. Right now, you're happy if you just get the plane back on the ground in one piece. Soon you'll gain confidence, and start to really enjoy the performance of your plane while it's in the air. There's no feeling quite like it!

4

Some Electric-Powered
Kits Reviewed

AIRTRONICS ECLIPSE

AIRTRONICS IS KNOWN PRIMARILY AS A company that produces excellent radio systems, in cooperation with Sanwa of Japan. But they also have a line of kits that are outstanding. Lee Renaud, founder of Airtronics, was a brilliant designer of sailplanes. He produced kits that were accurate and complete, and could be built into outstanding airplanes. Lee's family carries on the tradition with Airtronics.

The Olympic 650 is a classic Airtronics sailplane. Its two-meter wingspan is a convenient size, and its flying characteristics are slow and sweet—just what a low-time pilot needs. When Airtronics decided to produce an electric-powered airplane, they used the Olympic 650 as a basis for the design. The result is the Eclipse, one of the finest flying electric jobs you can get.

Construction. The Eclipse instructions start off with a complete list of all the tools you'll need. Everything else is in the box.

The fin and rudder are built up from sticks.

The structure is strengthened by using laminated balsa and spruce for the finpost. The stabilizer is also reinforced by spruce. The result is a tail section that's lighter than solid sheet but stronger than other built-up tails.

The wing is a beautiful piece of work. Thanks to the machine-cut ribs, it goes together easily. The Eclipse wing has a flat center section and upswept tips, rather than the conventional two V-shaped wing panels. This is easier to build for a beginner, in my opinion. The wingtips are removable, giving you three flat pieces for easy transportation.

The fuselage is built up from sheet sides. Because the Eclipse now uses a Leisure gear drive unit, the instructions have been changed to accommodate it. Check the addendum sheet, and make some notes on the plans where there are changes. The Leisure unit is much more reliable than the one originally supplied with the Eclipse, and it's even a little easier to install.

Jeff Troy's Eclipse on its way upstairs. This plane climbs fast, and when the engine stops and the prop folds back, it's one of the best sailplanes around.

The fuselage is set up to hold the wing on with rubber bands. It's easy to convert to a bolt-on wing if you like. You'll need to build a dowel into the leading edge of the wing center section, which will fit into a hole in Former F3. The rear of the wing center section should have a wide piece of balsa glued in between the two center ribs, flush with the trailing edge. You'll drill a hole through this area for the wing bolt, so it should be reinforced.

You can buy wing hold-down bolts and blocks that are already drilled and tapped in sets from SIG Manufacturing. Your hobby shop should have them in stock. They're quick and easy, and much cheaper than buying a set of taps!

Mount the wing hold-down block in the rear of the fuselage, with gussets underneath it. Make sure it doesn't interfere with the pushrods. Now mark the underside of the wing for the bolt hole. I do this with an old nylon bolt with the head cut off. I carve the top of the bolt to make a point, and cut a slot in it so I could turn it with a screwdriver. Then I thread it into the bolt hole. Pressing the wing down

Jeff Troy launches his Airtronics Eclipse. The motor is so powerful that no running start is required to get it in the air.

on it makes a dent that I can use to drill the hole in the wing trailing edge.

Covering. I covered my Eclipse with Oracover, a new plastic film sold by Hobby Lobby International. This is neat stuff, and very easy for a beginner to use. You apply it at a temperature that's so low the plastic film doesn't shrink at all. Stick it down to all the surfaces, pulling it fairly tight as you go. Then aim a heat gun at it and watch the wrinkles disappear.

Oracover goes over the solid sheet fuselage sides very easily, since it doesn't shrink while you're applying it. There's no tendency for the edges to pull back as the covering cools and the adhesive grabs. With a little Goldberg striping tape to hide the seams, even a beginner (or a hacker like me) can produce a neat covering job.

Radio and Motor Control. I used the Airtronics Vanguard four-channel radio in the Eclipse. It came with mini servos, which gave me a lot more room in the fuselage. It also has a small battery pack, which is more than enough to fly the Eclipse all day. Electronically, this is one of the best radios you can buy, and the price is very competitive.

Instead of permanently installing the Leisure seven-cell 800 MAh drive battery as shown on the plans, I held it in the fuselage with Velcro. I like to be able to take the battery out of the fuselage after a flight to let it cool more quickly. This also means I don't have to install a charging jack for the drive pack in the side of the firewall. And if I have a spare pack charged and waiting, I can go right back up again!

The Eclipse plans show you how to mount a

The Airtronics Eclipse is a sweet-flying sailplane that any beginner will enjoy. A Leisure Electronics power system with a folding prop is included in the kit.

servo-operated on-off switch for the motor. I prefer to use a speed controller with a geared motor system; it's easier on the gears when you turn on power slowly. Hobby Lobby's little Miniblitz controller fit nicely in the nose of the Eclipse, and gives me a small safety switch for the motor that mounts through the fuselage easily.

Flying. I am very impressed with the Leisure gear drive and Master Airscrew folding prop sup-

plied with the Eclipse. There are few better electric power systems anywhere, and they're just right for this airplane.

The Eclipse will launch from a standstill with a strong throw into the wind. Under power, climb is smooth and solid. It won't take you more than a minute to get up to the clouds.

After you shut down, the Eclipse really shows off its Airtronics bloodline. What a sailplane! I

The Eclipse carries its battery pack right behind the motor. To change packs, you remove the screw in the rear of the hatch cover.

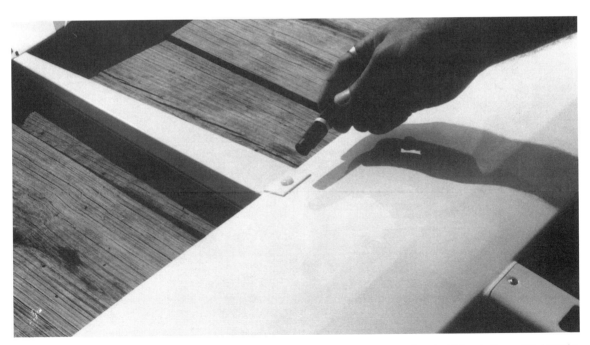

The Eclipse kit comes with parts for a wing held on with rubber bands, but you can easily adapt it to a bolt-on wing. I used a SIG nylon bolt and pre-tapped hold-down block.

The Eclipse wing has a flat center section and upswept tip panels. The outer panels unplug for easy carrying and storage.

The Eclipse fuselage is slim, but it has plenty of room for standard servos. The third servo at the front is for the motor on-off switch.

swear you could thermal this plane in the hot air arising from conversations in the pits.

When the time comes to land, set up your approach a good distance from the end of the runway. The Eclipse will glide a long way with the prop folded back, and you want to let it settle onto the runway, not spear it nose-first into the dirt to keep from overshooting.

The Eclipse is an absolutely delightful airplane. Any beginner can handle its gentle flying characteristics. Experienced pilots will appreciate its performance. And any model builder will be impressed by the quality and completeness of Airtronics kits. Introducing electric power to an Airtronics sailplane has led to a marriage made in heaven!

ASTRO FLIGHT MINI CHALLENGER

Astro Flight is the oldest company in the electric flight business. Not only have they been developing, selling, and promoting electric-powered planes for years, but they've worked on some famous full-scale planes. For example, the Solar Challenger (which flew the English channel using only solar cells for power) was powered by an Astro engine.

Astro Flight developed cobalt magnet motors for electric flight, which extended the power range of electric models considerably. They have consistently produced excellent chargers as well.

Astro's kit line is very good indeed. The wood is excellent, and all parts are cut very well. The plans are good, making it easier to get by with the sometimes-skimpy instructions in some of their older kits.

The little Astro Sport is a good small-field flier on inexpensive ferrite motors. It can be built with or without ailerons. I'm currently flying Astro's Partenavia Victor, a scale model powered by twin 05 Cobalt motors and 14 cells. It's a hot aerobatic performer with excellent power. I can do every aero-

The author prepares to launch his Astro Flight Porterfield Collegiate. This big, beautiful ship is powered by an Astro Cobalt 15 geared motor system, and turns a 13-inch prop.

Stacey Shope shows off the Mini Challenger at the beach. I couldn't persuade her to fly it!

Under the wing, the drive battery is taped to the bottom of the fuselage, and the receiver is Velcroed on top of it. The two micro servos are in the rear.

batic maneuver in the book for about four minutes, and still have enough power for a good approach and landing.

When I was selecting kits for this book, I faced a dilemma deciding on which Astro Flight kit to spotlight. My very favorite Astro kit, the Porterfield Collegiate, would be an excellent choice for a first-timer. It's big, with a 6-foot wingspan, and it flies nice and slow. It's not hard to build, even though the fuselage is built from sticks rather than sheet. The Porterfield uses a 15-size geared motor; mine flies on 12 cells and turns a 13-8 prop. This power package is a little more expensive than a beginner might want, but the flight performance of the Porterfield is well worth it.

I decided to feature the Astro Mini Challenger mainly because it is the newest Astro kit as of this writing, and it's aimed directly at beginners. Astro is going all-out to produce a kit that a beginner can afford, build, and fly. The Mini Challenger kit includes a Cobalt 035 motor and five-cell battery pack. There's even a special folding prop with Graupner scimitar blades included. This design is a smaller version of the contest-winning Astro Challenger, and retains much of the sparkling performance of its older brother while being easier for a beginner to build and fly.

The Mini Challenger is not the easiest beginner electric kit to build. Since the tail surfaces are built-up rather than solid sheet, and the wing leading edges are laminated from two pieces, you'll have to do some careful construction. But the instructions are perfectly adequate, and there's nothing here a typical beginner can't handle. Besides, the extra work gives you a racy-looking bird with wonderful flight performance.

Fuselage. Be careful to get the motor mount block glued in at the correct angle. This block is pre-drilled to fit the engine. Position the fuselage over the side view and use a glue that gives you a few minutes to eyeball the block into position.

The sheet fuselage sides are precisely cut. In

The forward fuselage houses the motor and the on-off switch. I secured the hatch with strips of SIG Supercoat Trim.

The Mini Challenger's tail surfaces are built from sticks. The elevator pushrod exits at the rear of the fuselage; the rudder pushrod needs a slot in the top just ahead of the fin.

fact, the cutting of all the wood in the kit is very impressive. Once the motor mount is in place, framing the fuselage is simple. Follow the instructions and you will end up with a straight fuselage. Be especially careful to keep the tail end square, so the stabilizer and fin will be correctly aligned.

Tail Surfaces. The tail pieces are built up of sticks, rather than sheet balsa. This takes more work than using pre-cut sheet pieces, but is much lighter. Pin the leading and trailing edges of each piece in place over the plans. Cut all connecting pieces slightly oversize and sand them to a perfect fit. I used Super Jet on all glue joints, but a thinner CyA like Jet or Hot Stuff will do the job well as long as the joints are perfect. If you're using thick CyA,

put a small drop on each end of the stick before you fit it in place. With thin CyA, fit the part and allow a drop of the glue to flow into the joint between the two pieces.

I drilled the holes for the rudder and elevator horns before covering. I almost always struggle with the tiny screws that hold the horns in place. A jeweler's screwdriver is essential for installing these. My friend Jeff Troy, who is a better model builder than I'll ever be, uses tiny socket-head screws instead of the slotted screws that come with the horns. Using an Allen wrench to tighten the screws rather than a standard screwdriver means the screwdriver can't slip off the screw and poke a hole in the covering.

Wing. To achieve a light wing, relatively thin hardwood strips are used for the spars. Vertical-grain balsa webs between each rib, glued to the spars, make a strong structure. Be sure to carefully fit each of these webs and make sure that they're firmly attached to the spars; it's less important to get them glued to the ribs, but it's helpful. I cut and fitted each web, then when it was the way I wanted it, I ran a line of Super Jet on the face of each spar and pressed the web into place. You can leave the webs slightly tall if you like; any part that sticks up above the spars can easily be sanded off.

The leading edges are made from two strips that are laminated together. This allows you to get that beautiful curve to the leading edge on the wingtips. I pinned the pieces tightly in place with no

                  was sat-
              the two
             CyA to
            lowly on
           il you've

r, sand it
allow you
Move the
ling edge
keep you
corner of

ager with
ventional
a good
Supercoat

ed on the wing and opaque White on the fuselage and tail.

Covering the wing can be done in three steps. First, the center section: Cover the bottom first, sealing the Supercoat carefully to each of the outer ribs. Supercoat is a low-temperature film; watch your iron temperature! (I use a Coverite iron and check the temperature with their pocket thermometer.) Top Flite's Trim Sealing Tool is also very helpful, especially in the corners at the bottom of the vertical fin.

Once the center section is covered, smaller pieces of Supercoat can be used to cover the outer

wing panels. Overlap the covering onto the center section about $1/8$ inch. Make sure this overlap is sealed all along its length. Supercoat shrinks very well, so you can concentrate on getting it stuck down at a lower temperature, then turn up the iron and shrink out the wrinkles.

Supercoat's adhesive side has a slight tack to it, so it's not a good idea to let it touch itself. Here's another hint for the transparent Supercoat: Don't get fingerprints or dust on the adhesive side! You can't clean it off, and it shows when you're finished.

Once the tail surfaces are covered, it's time to install the hinges. These surfaces are quite thin, so you have to be careful. My favorite hinges, SIG Easy Hinges, are definitely the ones to use here. Since you only have to cut a very thin slot for these, they'll save you a lot of trouble.

Radio Installation. Thanks to the slim fuselage, micro-size servos are essential. I used Futaba's Attack system designed for sailplanes; it comes with a small receiver pack, two micro servos, and a miniature receiver. This is an excellent radio that has served me well. Even the switch is small.

At this point you'll need to decide how you're going to turn the motor on and off. Astro Flight makes a solid state on-off control that simply plugs into the throttle channel of the receiver. I've had very good success with it. Because of the cobalt motor and five-cell battery pack, I don't recommend either the Futaba MCR-4A receiver or the Graupner Power Switch. Both of these power the receiver from the drive battery pack, and they're intended for packs no smaller than six cells.

In the nose of the plane, right behind the motor, I put the receiver battery pack. I used double-sided foam tape ("servo tape") to fasten the battery to the fuselage floor. Then I attached the on-off controller to the battery pack with servo tape. Finally I closed up the hatch with strips of white Supercoat trim material. You can't even tell the hatch is there!

I attached the five-cell drive battery pack to the fuselage floor under the wing, and stuck the receiver on top of it with servo tape. I mounted the receiver switch on the right slightly in front of the receiver. Finally, I servo-taped the servos to the rear of the compartment, one against each wall.

Flying. Since the battery pack isn't easily accessible, you have to figure on charging between flights instead of swapping packs. This is the one beef that I have with the Mini Challenger. To my mind, the ideal way to fly electric is with three battery packs: one flying, one charging, and one cooling down. In this case, because of the slim, high-efficiency fuselage, there's no bottom hatch to allow you to get at the battery. The sparkling performance makes up for this inconvenience. In fact,

if there's any kind of thermal activity around, the Mini Challenger will stay in the air plenty long enough on a single charge. It's much easier to build this way, too.

I started flying my Mini Challenger with a 7-4 wood prop. I got a very good climb, and good power-off performance, but I snapped a prop blade when I landed. A Cox 6-4 plastic prop was much better; it gave me a better climb than the bigger prop.

With the 7-4 Zinger prop I was getting about four and a half minutes of power from a charge. Changing to a 6-4 Zinger gave me a solid six min-

The Mini Challenger shows off its distinctive curved wingtips on this low pass with the power off and the prop blades folded back.

The Mini Challenger climbs out over the beach houses at Nags Head, NC. I love to take this compact sailplane along on trips; its docile handling makes flying from unfamiliar fields much easier.

utes of powered flight. That's enough for three or four climbs to altitude and a lot of gliding around. Cobalt motors do tend to drink the charge out of a pack faster than conventional ferrite motors.

When I reported all this to Bob Boucher of Astro Flight, he told me that he planned to include a special folding prop based on the Graupner scimitar blades with the production Mini Challenger. I immediately ordered one of these props from Hobby Lobby and slapped it on the 035 motor. Wow! This gave the best climbs and the longest motor runs of any I tried. Shutting off the motor flips the blades back flush with the fuselage, cleaning the plane for a smooth glide. The difference is noticeable—and, of course, there's not much chance of breaking a blade on a normal landing.

After several months of flying the Mini Challenger, I'm still delighted with it. For a sailplane with good thermal capability, it's remarkably compact. I've taken it on many trips and flown it in a lot of strange places, including the beach at Nags Head (that's *my* kind of windsurfing!).

If you want delightful electric performance in a compact package, check out the Astro Flight Mini Challenger. It's one of the nicest powered sailplanes around—just the thing for schoolyard or athletic field flying. It'll slow down and float for you, or turn sharply to stay in a thermal—couldn't be better!

COX ELECTRIC MALIBU

Cox Hobbies has been designing small airplanes for a long time. They are most famous for their .049 engines, which they have literally turned out in the millions. Cox distributes much of their wares through large retail stores rather than hobby stores; you've almost certainly seen some of their control line planes there. A hobby store is still the best place to buy the stuff, since the advice from the experts that you'll get is invaluable. But if you bought your Cox plane at a K-Mart, don't let that keep you from going to the local hobby shop for supplies for it! The hobby store will have what you need, and be able to tell you how to use it.

The Cox Electric Malibu is truly almost ready to fly. You don't even need glue to put it together!

The Electric Malibu is a kissing cousin of Cox's EZ-Bee trainer plane. The EZ-Bee uses a Cox .049 engine for power rather than the electric motor in the Malibu. Both planes are remarkably easy to assemble and fly. Obviously, I prefer the Malibu; starting the motor by throwing a switch is easier than tuning up a little .049—not to mention the lack of exhaust oil! On the other hand, the gas engine is capable of longer runs, and will keep the plane in the air longer. Take your pick.

The Electric Malibu is a remarkably complete package. You can buy it with or without the radio. If you buy it with the Cadet II radio in the package, it comes with the receiver, battery holder, and servos installed. You can literally assemble this version and have it flying in a hour.

A Cox Cadet radio system is the obvious choice for flying the Malibu. Another radio could be made to work without much trouble, but the servo holes in the fuselage are sized for the Cox servos.

I've had good luck with the inexpensive Cadet II system, but it has one problem: Each of its two sticks only moves in one direction. The Cadet III three-channel radio is vastly superior. It puts both rudder and elevator on a single stick that moves in two directions, which is much easier to control. Furthermore, since most RC planes are flown this way, you won't have to learn a new technique when you move on to a three- or four-channel airplane.

The Cadet III is an ideal system for many small airplanes. I especially like it in electric-powered planes, since the third channel can easily be used to turn the motor on and off.

The receiver is powered by four alkaline cells. Converting to rechargeable ni-cd cells is easy; just snap them into place in the holder. I don't recommend Radio Shack rechargeables, since I've found that they don't have as much capacity as other cells. Order some Sanyo cells from Ace RC; they're the best. You can convert the transmitter just as

There are molded pockets in the Malibu fuselage to hold the servos, receiver, and battery pack. The Deluxe version comes with radio already installed.

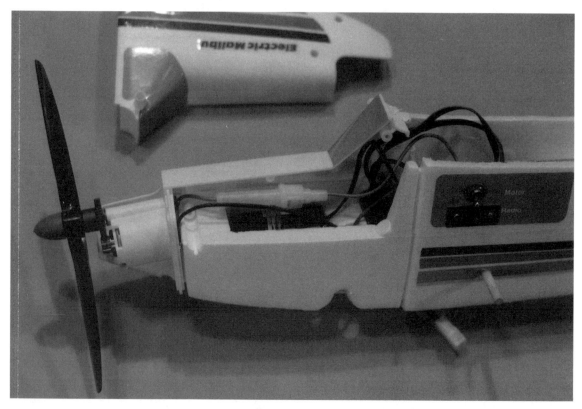

The plastic front of the Malibu is held in place with four screws. Slots in the plastic clamshell hold the motor mount in place. The receiver battery, fuse, and lead nose weight are in the nose section.

easily with eight ni-cd cells. The transmitter comes with a charging jack, so you can get into the ni-cd pack with a Cox, Airtronics or Futaba system charger. Charging the receiver pack is a bit more tricky. I generally do it by unplugging the switch lead into the receiver, turning the switch to on, and connecting a charger to the plug. You can get the appropriate plug from Cox, or you can jam-fit a three-pin male Deans connector into the plug contacts.

If you decide not to go with ni-cd batteries yet, be sure to note the amount of time the receiver is left on. Alkaline cells (DuraCells and the like) are fine for this sort of use, but they do run down. And unlike ni-cd cells, you can't easily test them to see how much capacity they have left. Fresh DuraCells should be good for three hours of receiver time. It's easier on the transmitter, since the meter will warn

you when the eight cells in the transmitter battery are running low.

The instructions describe a way that the Malibu can be flown with a single servo. This involves connecting the elevator pushrod to the rudder servo in such a way that up elevator is added whichever way the rudder is moved. In my experience, I've found that this method makes the model difficult to control. It's hard to get just the right amount of up in the turns when you have no control over the elevator. The end result is that you tend to gallop all over the sky, never quite getting the nose down onto a level heading. My advice is to pop for the second servo and have elevator control from the transmitter.

Assembly. The only place where it's necessary to use glue on the Malibu is joining the wing halves, and here it's optional. The wing halves are connected at the bottom of the root; fold them up and fasten them with a piece of tape across the center section, and the wing is ready. I put some epoxy in the joint just in case the tape decided to loosen up as it got dirty.

The forward fuselage is a clamshell of two plastic sections. It has to be opened up to put the receiver batteries in the holder.

Once you have the nose weight pieces and receiver battery in place, you secure the two nose piece halves with screws. The motor mount must fit tightly in slots in the front of the nose. This holds the motor firmly at the right angle of thrust offset, and gives you a strong nose structure to take abuse on landing.

The landing gear simply clips into place by sliding the gear into the slot in the lower fuselage and wedging it in with the plastic locking piece provided. You can get away with leaving the landing gear off, but since the Malibu needs a bit of nose weight anyway, it's best to install it.

The tailfeathers install without glue. Two threaded metal rods project from the vertical fin through holes in the stabilizer and out the bottom of the fuselage. Plastic nuts are threaded onto the projecting ends to keep the whole shebang in place.

The radio components come already installed if you buy the Deluxe version with the two-channel radio. If you need to install a radio, it certainly isn't hard; there are molded foam pockets for the receiver and servos. The pockets are sized for Cox Cadet servos. I really don't recommend using another radio system, although different servos could be bash-fitted into the holes. The Cox Cadet radio is light, compact, and efficient. As mentioned earlier, I strongly recommend the Cadet III single stick system.

Battery. The Malibu comes with its own battery. It's a special pack made of 250 MAh cells, for light weight. Fortunately, it also comes with its own charger, since there are few car-type chargers that can handle cells this small. The only problem with the included charger is that it doesn't slow-charge the pack, which is very helpful for getting the longest life and the most power from the pack.

You can solve this problem by getting a different charger. You could get a Metered Vari-Charger from Ace RC, which will not only slow-charge the drive battery, but the transmitter and receiver as well if you install ni-cd cells in them. Spending a bit more money will get you a charger with variable current, such as the Astro Flight AC/DC charger, which will fast-charge cells of several different sizes. This will also be very useful for more planes than the Malibu. The very best way to go is to get a peak detection charger that has a variable charge rate, such as the Novak Peak Plus. This will allow you to charge almost all different sizes of cells, up to seven-cell packs, at any rate you please. It even detects full charge and shuts itself off, and you can give your transmitter and receiver batteries a quick boost on the field.

Flying. There are two things to keep in mind when flying the Malibu. First, have you got a full charge in the battery pack? The very best way to be sure of this is to slow-charge the pack for 16 hours with a charger such as the Ace Metered Vari-Charger set at a rate of 250 milliamps. If you're using the Cox charger that came with the plane, charge the battery for 15 minutes as the instructions describe. Now grab the battery pack. Is it warm? If not, give it another five minutes. Check it every minute to see if the pack is warming up; at the first indication that it's getting warm, stop charging.

The second thing is the wind. If you can, fly the Malibu the first time in a dead calm. Gusty winds will push the plane around, and you'll naturally try to react, which can make the plane oscillate even further. Wait until the hours before sundown, when the winds are usually calm. Once you feel more proficient with the Malibu you can try it in light breezes, but it shouldn't be flown in a wind of much over 5 mph.

Plug in the battery, secure it, turn on the transmitter and receiver, and wiggle the controls. Make sure the rudder and elevator move in the right directions! As many years as I've been flying, I still check control movement before I take off. I get teased for this sometimes, but it sure makes me feel better.

Face into the wind (if there is any). Hold the

The Malibu's tail surfaces are held on by two long bolts coming out of the bottom of the fin. Plastic nuts thread onto the bolts where they come out the bottom of the fuselage.

Malibu overhead. Make sure the nose is pointed at the horizon. Don't try to do a javelin-throw launch with the nose pointed up; you'll almost certainly throw it into an attitude from which you won't be able to recover.

Switch on the motor, and take a few fast steps forward. The Malibu will start to lift out of your hand. Let it. Grab your transmitter and concentrate on keeping the wings level and establishing a gentle climb.

To turn, bank the plane with rudder. As you see the nose drop, pull the elevator stick back to keep the plane level. As it comes around, apply opposite rudder to level the wings, and release the up elevator gradually. Remember, the rudder banks the plane, and the elevator does the turning. Keep your turns wide and work on learning when to apply elevator. You'll soon have the Malibu flying smoothly.

The battery will take you up to a good altitude, and you might even have trouble hearing when the motor starts to run down. If the plane needs more and more elevator to keep it level, you're starting to run out of battery. Set up your landing approach, concentrating on keeping the plane level. If you dive at the ground and then pull up, you'll have so much speed that the Malibu will go right back up in the air. Try to let it settle on its own, and keep your wings level. It's a lot easier than it sounds.

The Cox Electric Malibu is an excellent first-time airplane. It's one of the simplest ready-built planes available, and certainly one of the easiest to assemble! Flying characteristics are excellent. The foam construction is easy to repair in the event of a crash, but the Malibu flies so gently that you're not going to do much crashing.

DAVEY SYSTEMS

Davey Systems originally made their reputation with a fine line of sailplane kits. It seemed like a natural progression a few years ago when Davey started producing products for electric flight. Now they have one of the best ranges of electric kits in the business, not to mention a line of electric flight accessories.

Davey's electric kits are available with or without an 075-size motor and switch harness. This is a very good motor for seven-cell packs; it's got more power than the stock 05-size motors you find included with some other kits. I've found that the best prop for a Davey 075 is a 7-4, which is an inch larger than the 6-4s usually used on ferrite motors. They're a good choice for converting small gas-powered models to electric, since they'll pull a heavier weight.

Davey sells an Amp Meter designed for electric motors. Most meters that you can buy in electronics stores don't go up to the 20 or so amps that

Retired General Dick Dean built this beautiful LeCrate and covered it with transparent film to show off his work. This is one of the best-flying trainers available.

The LeCrate fuselage is built from sticks, and has plenty of room for a radio. Dick Dean used a curved piece of aluminum sheet for the nose section cover.

an electric motor can draw. Davey's meter plugs in between the motor and the rest of the power system; it's available with either Tamiya or Sermos connectors.

With the Davey meter, you can directly test the current draw of your motor with different props. You can check your speed controller to make sure it's delivering plenty of current by comparing the amps delivered to the motor with the controller in the circuit to the reading you get when the battery is plugged straight into the motor. It will even help you spot switches and connectors that are building up resistance and robbing the motor of current. No serious electric flier should be without one of these meters.

LeCrate

Davey's electric kits are excellent designs. Two of my favorites were designed by the old master himself, Bill Winter. I can claim some responsibility for getting Bill interested in electric flight back in the late '70s. He talked back then about the ideal electric airplane: light, easy to build, good power-off glide, good climb. The magic goal in those days was to make a 20-minute flight, without thermal assist, on standard motors and batteries. Bill came up with the LeCrate, a sweet little high-wing plane that will consistently do 12 to 15 minutes even in the hands of a raw beginner.

Davey's translation of Bill's LeCrate into a kit is a gem. It is undoubtedly the sweetest-flying elec-

You can mount the battery pack permanently in the LeCrate fuselage, and charge it through a jack. Or you can build a hatch in the bottom and use replaceable batteries.

My brother Richard Pratt built this LeCrate and is still enjoying it three years later. He even puts a miniature camera in it and takes pictures looking out the side window!

Bill Winter's remarkable Heron is designed for all-out electric performance. Davey Systems's kit of the Heron is an excellent choice for experienced builders, and can give you 20-minute flights.

Many Davey Systems electric kits use an adjustable engine mount that makes it easy to try different engines. This is the Caliph, a sweet-flying low-wing trainer plane.

tric a beginner can build. It's economical, since the deluxe version comes with motor, prop, and wiring harness, and it flies just fine on common RC car battery packs. You can improve the performance by buying the standard kit and using a Leisure LT50 geared motor system on seven-cell battery packs.

LeCrate was designed for a beginner to build, so there are some compromises. Bill turned himself loose to build an optimized electric job, this time designed around the big (11 – 12 inch) folding propellers that were just becoming available. The result was the Heron, which Davey has recently released in kit form. Its lifting stab and swept leading edge give it spectacular performance, and the long nose allows a long prop to fold back completely. The Heron isn't for beginners. For one thing, the motor needs to be mounted near the midpoint of the plane, and an extension shaft is needed to the prop. I built mine with a brand-new Leisure sailplane gear drive unit. This has a molded housing for the extension shaft, and the shaft is supported by ball bearings. Once you have the power system figured out, the Heron isn't a hard build for an experienced modeler. And it's well worth the trouble. The Heron makes the magic 20-minute dead-air flights commonplace.

Eindecker

Davey's newest electric kit is the little semi-scale Eindecker. This plane is a departure from the usual for this book, since it's not really a gentle-flying trainer. But if you're looking for snappy performance, or you're an experienced gas flier who wants to tool around the sky, the Eindecker is for you. On seven cells with the stock motor, it has just

Davey's Eindecker is a cute little semi-scale electric with snappy performance. You can build it for either electric power or a Cox .049 gas engine.

The Eindecker's fuselage is open at the rear, which makes it easy to route the pushrods and antenna. Tail surfaces are precut sheet balsa.

as much ''go'' as a sport .049 job. In fact, the plans show how to install a Cox .049 if you want.

Wing. The spars are *just* long enough . . . measure them carefully when you cut them! It's a good idea to cut the spars, leading edge, and trailing edge to length before you start assembling the wing; this lets you do the cutting right over the plan. Cut the outer spars so that they extend through the wingtip rib and flush against the W-2 rib in the center section.

It isn't too clear in the instructions that you make yourself two W-2 ribs by cutting $1/16''$ off the outside edge of two W-1 ribs. I found a good way to

sand the ribs to size: I stacked the two W-1 ribs with the $3/32''$ rib that's pre-cut for the very center of the center section. I put a couple of pins through the three ribs to keep them together, and trimmed and sanded the two W-1 ribs to the size of the smaller $3/32''$ rib. You have to line them up with the spar slots. Don't cut off the trailing edges.

Test-fit the trailing edge to be sure you have it right-side-up. It should fit flush against the rear of each rib. Bevel the outer tip of each trailing edge before you glue it down, so the wingtips will fit properly. Cut the wingtips from one of the $3/16''$ square sticks.

With the outer panels propped up at the correct dihedral angle, check to be sure that the bottom spars make a good contact with the bottom spar in the center section. Sand if necessary. Then apply glue to the bottom spars and check the wing angle again. Glue in the dihedral brace before the glue on the bottom spars sets, so that you can make last-minute adjustments. It's easier than it sounds.

The instructions don't mention the $1/4''$ by $3/16''$ piece that is glued into the rear of the center section before the top sheeting goes on. It's there on the plans, though, so don't leave it out. Butt the top rear center sheeting against this piece; it can easily be sanded to the right shape after you remove the wing from the building board.

The instructions also fail to mention the tip gussets that glue in between the spars and the $3/16''$ square wingtip piece. This starts life as a gusset the same size as the others. Trim off the point

and sand it at an angle to make a good fit between the last W-1 rib and the tip. Make sure the gusset is firmly glued to both spars.

Fuselage. Building a fuselage from sticks isn't hard. In fact, it's fun! See our discussion of the Leisure Amptique for a description of my favorite stick-building methods.

Don't put in the gussets until after you've glued the stick framework to the sheet sides. This lets you get the gussets flat against the sheet sides and firmly glued to them.

The sheet sides will be just a little oversize. Sand them down to the outlines of the sticks.

The thin ply reinforcing plates that glue into the very rear of the fuselage are oversize. Fit them so that they're flush with the side the stab will mount on, and trim off the part that projects over the top.

Note that when you glue in F2 it has to be positioned so that you can glue in a crosspiece underneath it. This leaves F2 projecting a tiny bit above

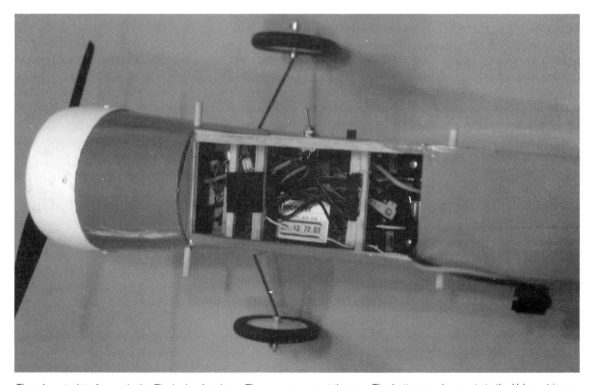

There's not a lot of room in the Eindecker fuselage. Three servos are at the rear. The battery pack mounts to the Velcro strips on struts over the receiver.

the top of the fuselage; a few swipes with a sanding block brings it out square.

Motor Mount. Cutting the hole in the ply firewall for the rolled tube motor mount is a bit of a pain. The right tools make it a lot easier. I started by transferring the circle from the plans to the ply firewall. I turned the plans over, and positioned the firewall so that it was perfectly centered under the drawing showing the motor hole. Then I brushed a little dope thinner on the back of the plans, and hit it with my sealing iron for a few seconds. This process smells bad, but it makes a nice blueprint on the firewall.

I drilled several $1/4''$ holes around the inside of the motor hole. Then I chucked a Robart Carbide Cutter drum into my drill and used it to cut between the holes. Finally I used the cutter to sand the hole out to the outlines.

Next I wrapped the $1/32''$ ply motor tube material around the motor and cut it to the correct length. I test-fitted the motor and ply tube in the engine mount hole; the hole was too small. A few passes with the carbide drum took care of it. Be sure to work all the way around the hole at each pass to be sure it stays straight. Once I had a good fit, I glued the ply tube to the firewall, being careful not to get glue on the motor.

Finishing the Fuselage. The pre-cut side pieces make it much easier to finish the fuselage construction. They fit very nicely against the curved sides of the firewall. Dampen the balsa side pieces on the outside and let the water soak in before you attempt to bend them; this will help keep the sides from cracking. If they do crack, just glue the crack with thin CyA. Install the sides, then sheet the top.

Cowl. The Eindecker has a round cowl around its radial engine. To put that in a kit means making an expensive molded plastic or fiberglass piece. Instead, the instructions tell you how to make one from the bottom of a one-liter pop bottle.

Those plastic soda bottles have a reinforcement around the bottom that makes a perfect Eindecker cowl. The reinforcement is glued in three places; I worked it free with a long screwdriver. Then I cut the piece lengthwise with a pair of scis-

sors. Finally, I used a heat gun to soften the plastic and, using the front of the fuselage as a guide, bent and trimmed the plastic piece to shape.

Pushrods. No holes need to be cut in the rear. The threaded rods project out the opening in front of the stabilizer.

Davey thoughtfully includes Phillips-head screws for the control horns. This helps keep your screwdriver from slipping off the screw and poking a hole in the rudder or elevator.

Radio Installation. If you use an .049 engine on this plane, there's more than enough room in the fuselage for the radio. However, the electric version is a tight fit. I had no problem stuffing everything in under the wing, but it took a little planning.

First of all, use a radio system with mini- or micro-size servos and a small battery pack. I used the Ace Silver Seven receiver, a 250 milliamp-hour battery pack, and Ace Bantam Midget servos. I fitted the servos, receiver, and battery with double-sided foam tape. The battery pack fit in nicely in front of the ply landing gear plate; be careful not to obstruct the air inlet hole under the motor. The servos need to go as close to the bottom of the fuselage as possible. Once they're in, drill holes in the rear fuselage former in line with the output arm of each servo for the pushrods to come through. Now attach the receiver to the fuselage bottom, and fit the switch through the lower right side of the fuselage.

I put the motor switch on the right side of the fuselage, low down on the side.

The drive battery pack goes above all this. The only size pack that will fit is a seven-cell pack of 800 MAh cells (or SR Batteries' 1250 MAh cells). I used leftover $3/16''$ square pieces to make two battery supports. These extend across the fuselage at the front and back of the radio compartment. I glued three small pieces of $3/16''$ square to each battery support to give me a place to put two pieces of Velcro. The Velcro is all that's needed to hold the battery in place.

Test-fit the wing with the battery in place. It might be necessary to move the battery supports down a little to make sure the battery doesn't keep the wing from seating.

Flying. The Eindecker is a snappy little performer with plenty of power. Don't set up the controls to move too far, or it'll be too sensitive.

It'll rise out of your hand after a few running steps. Loops and snap rolls are crisp. You'll like the way the Eindecker toots around the sky. With the power off, the glide is fairly steep, so set up your landing approach while you still have some power.

Faster and snappier than most small electrics, the little Eindecker is one of the most fun electrics you can fly.

FUTABA PROFESSOR

Of all the planes I evaluated for this book, the Futaba Professor is one of my very favorites. My Prof has more flight time on it than many of the other planes in the workshop. One reason for this is its utter simplicity. All I have to do to go flying is rubber-band on the wing, strap a fresh battery into the compartment on the bottom of the fuselage, and grab the transmitter. This is what electric convenience is all about!

Another reason is that the compact little Professor is so portable—it lives in the back of my van and comes out when the weather is nice. But most of all, the Prof has such lovely flying characteristics that it's a pleasure just to tool around the sky.

As I've mentioned before, the phrase "almost ready-to-fly" is horribly abused. In some cases, it really means "almost ready to spend two weeks building." But in the Professor's case, you can believe it. I assembled my Professor while I was on vacation, using just what was in my tool kit. It took two hours. I didn't have a micro switch for on-off control with radio, so I set it up with only the external switch. This isn't a great way to fly if you're a beginner, since you can't land until the battery quits, but I wanted to fly it that day.

The only battery around was a six-cell 1200 MAh pack that had been in an RC car for years. I took it out of the car, peak-charged it, put it in the Prof, and tossed it in the air. It hooked a thermal within two minutes. Seventeen minutes later I brought it down and landed it within 10 feet of the lawn chairs where my brother Dick and I were

The Professor is one of the finest almost-ready-to-fly airplanes you can buy. It comes with motor, gear drive, prop and spinner already installed.

relaxing; his Electra was up for its second flight of the day. We traded transmitters, he put one of his packs in the Professor, and up it went again—for 10 minutes this time. Now, that's my kind of flying!

Radio Selection. You can use any aircraft radio in the Professor, as long as you have micro-size servos for it. Futaba sells the ideal system for the plane, the Attack with 4NBL/MCR receiver. As we discussed earlier, this radio comes with a speed controller and battery eliminator circuit in the receiver. You will have throttle-like control of the motor speed. More important, there is no need to carry a battery pack strictly for the receiver; circuitry in the receiver shuts the motor off when the main battery is getting low, giving you plenty of receiver power after there isn't enough for the motor.

If you use a radio other than the Attack 4NBL, you'll need a receiver battery. You should get one no longer than 250 MAh to save weight. I used a Futaba Conquest system with mini servos and a 200 MAh battery pack from SR Batteries.

Construction. The Professor is made from lightweight plastic shells that are laminated onto a wooden crutch. The tail surfaces are foamboard, and the wing is the same stuff bent over a wooden skeleton. The result is a remarkably light airplane that's almost completely prefabricated. This is one of very few ARFs that are just as light as a plane that you build. It shows in the performance, too.

The instructions that come with the Professor are well-illustrated—which is fortunate, because the English translations of the text are a little, uh, prosaic. If you wonder why the instructions occasionally refer to the wing as the "main blade," it's because the Japanese company that makes the Professor, Hirobo, also makes the famous Shuttle helicopter kit. You'll also get a chuckle out of phrases such as "Adhering slip-off between right and left wings may give a great influence on the flying performance." This isn't a big problem, since each assembly step has a detailed illustration; even the screws are drawn full-size for easy identification. This machine is so thoroughly prefabricated that the pictures are really all you need.

The wing halves are beautifully built. All you have to do is glue them together with the wing joiner in the slot. I marked the joiner in the center and super-glued it into one wing panel, to make sure it didn't slip farther into one panel when I put the two together.

Be sure that you cover the whole of the wing root with epoxy; there should be a solid glue joint on the entire mating surface. The only criticism I have of the kit is that I wanted more epoxy than came with it.

Don't leave out the plastic shield that goes over the center section of the wing. This keeps the rubber bands from digging into the lightweight wing structure. I used Super Jet to attach these—a light squiggle on the inside to secure them, and a second application to seal down the edges.

Eyeball the tail surfaces carefully and adjust them before the epoxy hardens to make sure they're perpendicular. It's helpful to mount the wing and look at the plane from the back while doing this.

The motor comes already in place, mounted with rubber bands. If you don't use the 4NBL/MCR receiver you'll need to dismount it and solder connectors onto the wiring for the motor control you're using.

Radio and pushrod installation is simple, just as shown in the illustrations. I always hate attaching control horns, since my screwdriver always seems to slip off the bolt head and poke a hole in the surface next to it. Work slowly and carefully, and always pre-drill holes for the bolts. Twirling a drill bit in your fingers will do the job nicely.

The instructions in my kit had an addendum sheet showing a simplified method of mounting the battery. I simplified it further by leaving off the body mount post and battery hatch cover. I get better battery cooling with the cover off, and it's much less hassle. The neat little releaseable tie wrap holds any common size pack securely, making the hatch cover unnecessary.

Flying. The wing hold-down dowels are a bit short, so you might be tempted to use only one rubber band on each side to hold the wing on. Use at least two on each side. I recommend that you cross the rubber bands, running from the left front to the right rear and vice versa. This way, they are less likely to slip off the dowels. To be *really* safe, you can take two smaller rubber bands and slip them over the dowels from left to right, so the big rubber bands can't go anywhere.

The Prof has plenty of power to rise right out of your hand, so launching is simple. Take a few steps and push it forward, straight and level. Fly it up to a comfortable altitude and start making turns. A little up elevator in the turns is all it takes. The Prof will pull itself out of a spiral dive very nicely if it has enough altitude. This is another plane that knows how to fly better than you and I do!

With the control linkages set up as shown on the instructions, you have plenty of rudder to turn sharply. The plane may feel a bit sensitive on the controls. If you find yourself overcontrolling and kicking the Prof all over the sky, move the clevises to the outermost holes of the control horns on the rudder and elevator. Try to make your control inputs smooth, and think ahead of the plane. The Professor makes this easy.

If you're a rank beginner, or you don't feel like building a plane, this is the model for you. It flies better than any other ready-built plane I've flown, and is one of the simplest to assemble. The Professor will get you to flight school fast, and will make sure you enjoy it when you get there.

GOLDBERG MIRAGE 550

It's a perfect evening, about an hour before sundown and not another soul in the park. The Ori-

The Mirage from Carl Goldberg Models is one of the finest Electric trainers available, Motor, prop and spinner are included.

Goldberg's Electra was the kit that started the electric flight explosion. It's still one of the best kits around for the beginner.

oles are leading the Yankees by three in the eighth on the car radio, and I'm at about 150 feet over the soccer field. I throttle back to one click below half and check the elevator trim—nice and level. I trim in a tiny bit of left rudder, set the transmitter on the ground, and start my stopwatch. Three and a half minutes later I pick the tranny back up and nudge the plane back overhead; it hasn't lost any altitude, but it's circling over the trees. Back overhead, I set up the same circle and put the transmitter down. Two minutes later the plane seems to be sinking a bit, so I stop the watch and take over. Power off, procedure turn, line up for final, and she's floating. On impulse I give it full throttle, and darned if there

isn't a little climb left! I get back upstairs, turn downwind, shut off the motor, and cruise into my turn onto final. Up elevator slows the ship into the nicest three-point you'd ever want to see. Yeah!

That was my third flight with the Goldberg Mirage. The plane is set up just as it comes from the box, with the exception of a Hobby Lobby Miniblitz speed controller and a seven-cell pack of 1800 milliamp cells from SR Batteries. The real kicker to this story is that my seven-minute warning timer had gone off *before* I started my hands-off circling routine—the flight totaled 14 minutes!

There is something very special happening with the Goldberg Mirage. It has splendid perform-

Brian Pratt shows his approval of the Goldberg Mirage. This is one of the best-flying trainers you can get, and one of the easiest to build.

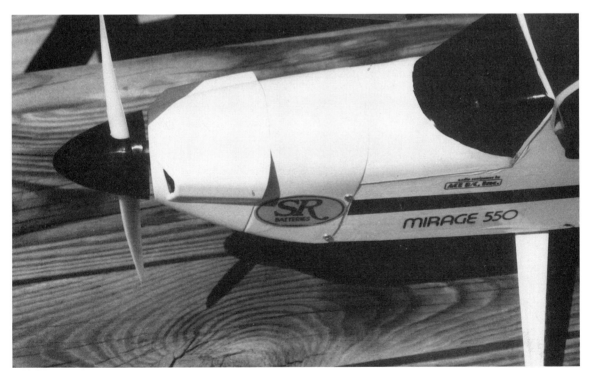

The Mirage comes with a motor, propeller, and spinner. The two-piece molded cowl fits over a molded plastic windshield/nose cover.

ance in a package that's easy to build, but so do some other planes we've talked about. I haven't quite hit on what makes the Mirage so special, but something about the way it flies really grabs me. It might be the Mirage's sleek looks, or its relatively compact size, or its convenient layout. Whatever, the Mirage stands out from the pack.

Construction. Each major assembly (tail, wing, fuselage) begins with an illustration of all the parts required for that step. It includes a drawing of the needed die-cut sheets, with all the parts called out. This keeps you from accidentally throwing away parts that fall out and aren't needed in the step you're doing at the moment—nice touch!

Keep a ruler handy to help you measure and locate the right strips. They are packaged logically; all elevator strips are banded together, for example. So don't take 'em out of the bundles until you're sure what you want is in that bundle.

Thanks to nicely die-cut tip and center pieces, building the built-up tail surfaces is very easy. Cut the sticks slightly oversize and sand them to an exact fit. Work carefully and you'll have a very sturdy tail structure that's much lighter than solid wood.

When you drill for the hinges, here's a tip: Make a stop for your drill bit by wrapping a piece of masking tape around it. This will give you a visual reference for exactly how deep the bit is into the piece you're drilling, and help keep you from poking a hole out of the side of the fin or rudder. I use a small cordless electric drill on low speed for this kind of precision work.

Fuselage. The fuselage assembles quickly, thanks to the solid sheet sides. The die-cut pieces fit together smoothly. All you have to do is run a bed of Super Jet glue around the joints, and your fuselage is done. To make it pretty, take a small

I used an Ace RC Olympic V radio system in my Goldberg Mirage. The kitchen timer Velcroed to the transmitter warns me when the battery is getting tired.

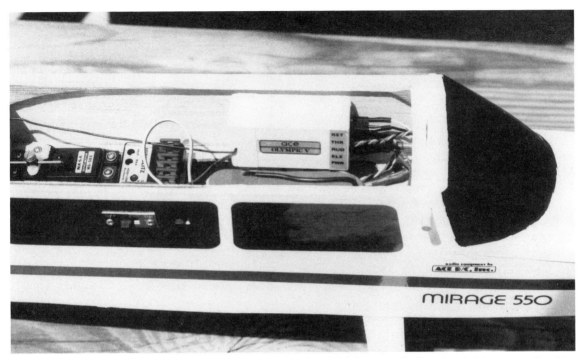

The Mirage has plenty of room for radio components. I mounted the Miniblitz controller just ahead of the servos. The drive battery is accessible through a hatch in the bottom.

sanding block and round off the corners. Smooth it all down with light sandpaper. Remember, covering a part doesn't hide flaws, it accentuates them.

Final Assembly. Don't permanently attach the cowl until you get the motor in place. Put the spinner on, adjust the cowl angle until it looks right, then drill the holes through the cowl corners and fix it with the screws included.

It was real nice of Goldberg to include a special long Allen wrench to attach the prop and spinner to the engine shaft! It makes life a lot easier.

Radio Installation. Installing the radio is simple. The die-cut radio tray fits any standard system. I used the Ace RC Olympic 5 system, which has some of the best electronics you can buy.

The instructions show you how to use a third servo to set up an on-off switch for the motor. This works fine, but in order to get flights like I've had you'll need proportional motor control. I ordered a Miniblitz speed controller from Hobby Lobby, and wired it to the throttle channel of the Ace receiver.

The Ace Olympic 5 system comes without servos, and I only had to buy two for this setup.

I found that the Miniblitz controller may "burp" momentarily when you switch it on. This gives a slight twitch to the prop—surprising, but not dangerous.

Flying. The Mirage is one of the sweetest-flying planes around. Pick calm air for your first flights; the Mirage can penetrate winds of 5 to 7 miles per hour, but it's a lot more fun in quiet winds.

I particularly like the Mirage's belly hatch for access to the battery compartment. If you have a field box with a stand on top of it, you can flip the plane over and swap batteries without removing the wing. The Robart Super Stand is handy for this—and cheap, too.

The Mirage is a fine kit, with fine instructions. It's complete, well made, and easy to build. And the way it flies would make Carl Goldberg himself proud.

GREAT PLANES

If you're a beginner who's never even been near a model airplane, you need a trainer plane with good instructions. Fortunately, there are several kits that have them.

PT-Electric

Some of the best instructions are the ones in the PT-Electric, written by the designer, Jim Schmidt. They will take you all the way through the building process, and teach you a lot on the way.

Another outstanding feature of the PT-Electric is the completeness of the kit. All you need is an inexpensive four-channel system with three servos, a battery pack, and a charger.

This is a kit that has been designed for light weight, but it is still remarkably easy to build.

That's engineering. You'll learn a lot from this plane in the process of building, and be ready to tackle just about anything else for your second plane.

Fuselage. Unlike some ''slab sided'' gas-powered trainers, the PT-Electric is almost all open structure. That means that there is a big bundle of sticks in this kit. You'll save yourself a lot of trouble if you do as it suggests in the instruction book: Measure and mark each stick before you start construction. A ruler graduated in 64ths and a super-fine point felt-tip pen are necessary for this job.

The larger die-cut pieces all have lightening holes cut in them. Fortunately, the die-cutting is excellent, so all of those circular pieces come out easily. Just to be certain, I took my Tee-Bar with light grit sandpaper and sanded the underside of each die-cut piece. They have to be smoothed off anyway sooner or later, and it's easy to do it before

The Great Planes PT-Electric is an easy kit to build, and a docile flier. It's an excellent choice for your first airplane.

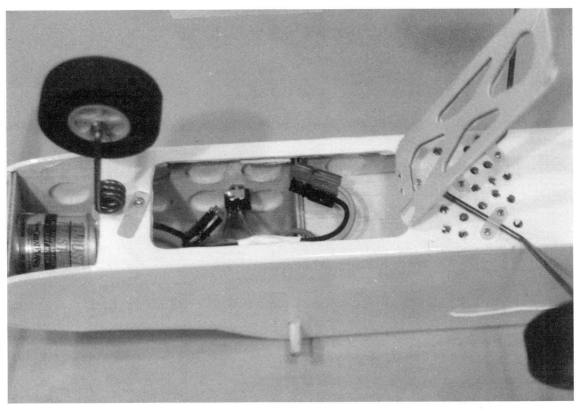

The PT-Electric has a belly hatch for the drive battery pack. The motor switch harness is pre-wired, and parts are included for on-off control from a third servo.

gluing the pieces together—a few swipes and the pieces fall right out.

The fuselage forward piece is held down over the plans, and the rear longerons are cut to length and glued into slots in the piece. This is like building rubber-powered models! I enjoy this kind of construction. Cut all your pieces slightly oversize and sand them to the exact shape of the plans. Take a little time to do an artistic job here, and you'll have a plane to be proud of.

The fuselage formers all have tabs that fit into slots in the sides. You assemble the whole fuselage dry. Inserting the die-cut plywood fuselage bottom squares the whole structure. Look it over to make sure all the parts are tight together, and run Super Jet over all the joints.

When you pull the tail of the fuselage together, don't try to get the tail post pieces to glue flat together; just stick them together along their rear edges. The stab platform and fuselage bottom pieces will fit between the posts.

Once the fuselage was together, I sanded it all over with a Tee-Bar and light grade paper. The more you sand it, the better it'll look when the covering goes on.

Tail. The tail surfaces are built up from sticks and die-cut pieces. It's easy; the instructions are well-illustrated, so just follow them in sequence.

I like to cut sticks slightly long and sand them until they're a perfect fit over the plans. If you try to cut a stick to the precise length, sooner or later one of them will be short—and it's mighty hard to make them longer!

I substituted SIG Easy Hinges for the plastic hinges supplied with the kit. These require no preparation or drilling. Just cut the hinge slots, fit

There's plenty of room for the radio in the PT-Electric fuselage. The servos are at the rear; the third servo controls the motor on-off switch.

the Easy Hinges in, and when you have the surfaces the way you want them, apply a drop of thin CyA glue to the top and bottom of each hinge. The Easy Hinges soak up the glue and wick it into the wood, providing a really solid joint. You can't get them out if you want to, so be *sure* you're ready to permanently hinge the surfaces before applying the glue!

Motor Installation. Stuffing the motor and wiring into the front of the plane is simple, as long as you do it before you sheet the top or bottom of the forward end of the fuselage. Stick to the sequence in the instructions!

I used some scrap balsa from one of the die-cut sheets to make a spacer that I glued underneath the microswitch. This made it easier for the yellow pushrod to contact the switch squarely.

I like the engine mounting system; it's simple and strong. When you drill the die-cut ply piece F-1B, do it from the back of the piece and work very slowly. If you try to run the drill through quickly, you could lose pieces of the outer ply.

Covering. I used SIG Supercoat iron-on film and trim material on the PT-Electric. Supercoat is very light, which is always a useful feature for electric planes. It's also a low-temperature film, so it's easier to wrap around corners and seams don't show as much. Follow the instructions that come with the film and set your iron with a thermometer. If you have one, shrink open areas with a heat gun. I opened up a hole in the covering over one wing panel by leaving the iron on it too long. Fortunately, the thin Supercoat seams very well, so I was able to make an almost-invisible patch.

Remove the landing gear and switches from fuselage exterior before covering. Iron strips down over the tail joints before covering the tail. Be sure to cut out all ventilation holes.

Flying. The PT-Electric flew as advertised for me: easy launch right out of my hand, slow flight, gentle turns, and landings that make a beginner look good. It doesn't climb like a rocket on six cells, so plan to fly straight and level on your first flight and don't worry about putting it out of sight.

After a satisfying first flight on a six-cell Sanyo pack, I decided to try a seven-cell pack of SR cells. I plugged it in, closed the hatch, turned on the radio, threw the motor switch, and hit the throttle—nothing. So I secured the plane upside-down in a holder, opened the hatch, and wiggled the connectors. That got me power to the motor, but popped the fuse in the process. Off to a local auto parts store for a new 20-amp fuse!

I discovered that the fuse holder really clamps the fuse in there; it took a pair of pliers to get it out. With a new fuse in place, I plugged in a seven-cell pack of SR 1800 MAh cells and headed out to the park. The PT-Electric flew out of my hand before I had taken two steps, and climbed with authority! I was up to comfortable altitude almost immediately, and the plane was almost out of sight in three minutes. When I shut the motor off, I trimmed the plane for a nice glide by adding two clicks of up elevator; no rudder was necessary. When we cruised back down, I hit the power and up we went again—and again! By the time I finally decided that the batteries were pooped and set up my landing approach, the flight had lasted over 12 minutes.

One of the nicest things about this plane is the way it flies. There's very little trim change when you shut off the motor; in fact, I left it set up in glide trim and simply controlled it under power by adding a little bit of down stick when the nose pointed up too far. The nose hardly drops in a powered turn. I've never seen it stall or snap. The glide is lovely, almost as flat as a sailplane. In other words, the PT-Electric won't hand you any unpleasant surprises. It knows how to fly, and loves to do it.

I would be cautious about flying the PT-Electric in a strong, gusty wind. You'll spend more time wrestling the lightly loaded plane around, and you won't have any fun. Go out when the wind is 5 mph or less—in other words, when flags are not standing straight out from the flagpole. Launch into the wind, and when you set up your approach, do it downwind. Practice gliding in to a landing while you're high in the air and have plenty of battery power to go back upstairs. It's also a good idea to land before you have to, so your batteries aren't too flat to pull you around for another approach.

The PT-Electric is a definite winner. Beginners will appreciate the beautiful instructions. The light weight of the craft makes it an excellent flier. I do recommend seven cells, but the PT will fly adequately on six.

ElectroStreak

Don't let anyone tell you that electric planes are all powered sailplanes or slow-flying antiques. There are electric planes out there that can fly any maneuver in the book, or keep up with a .40-powered racing plane.

The first commonly available kit to prove this point was the ElectroStreak from Great Planes Manufacturing. This is a small, sleek little beauty with aerobatic performance that will interest any Pattern flier. I wouldn't recommend it as your first RC airplane. Not because of the building; the ElectroStreak is easy to build, with excellent instructions. But this is definitely *not* a trainer plane! It goes where you point it, so you'd better know where you want it to go. If you enjoy flying aerobatics and most of the electrics you see are too tame for you, try an ElectroStreak.

The ElectroStreak whizzes by at full power. Aerobatics were never this fun—or this quiet—before.

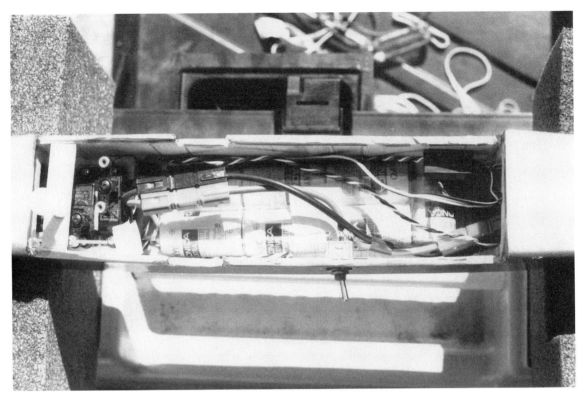

The ElectroStreak's seven-cell battery pack attaches to the fuselage floor with Velcro. Two micro servos are tucked in at the rear.

The Kit. The ElectroStreak kit is complete with motor, prop, and spinner. It's designed tightly around this motor, so I strongly recommend that you start out with it. Trying to hop it up with a Cobalt 05 or a racing-wound car motor is likely to give you nothing more than a shorter battery run.

You'll like the engineering. All die-cutting is clean, and construction goes quickly. Because there isn't much room in the fuselage, the rudder is controlled by pull-pull cables rather than a pushrod. I was a little concerned when the time came to install them, but it turned out to be a simple job.

Radio Equipment. The ElectroStreak requires a micro-sized radio system. A Cannon Super Micro system is ideal, since it weighs several ounces less than anything else available. I opted to use a Futaba Conquest system with micro receiver and servos, since they are more widely available.

The Futaba MCR-4A system would be a very good choice for the ElectroStreak. Since it doesn't require a receiver battery, it's easy to install and light. The only downside of using it is the auto-cut-off circuit, which will cut off the motor with quite a bit of capacity left. This is designed to make it possible to thermal a plane for 10 or 20 minutes after the battery runs down, but you're not going to be thermaling an ElectroStreak unless you're in the middle of a desert!

My system uses a 200 MAh battery pack and three servos. I Velcroed the battery pack to one side of the nose section forward of the battery compartment.

For control, I decided on a simple on-off switch. I installed the new switch made by JoMar using surface-mount electronics. This is a little board about the size of a square potato chip. The connectors are the biggest thing on it! It weighs almost nothing, and has worked beautifully. I Velcroed it to the other side of the nose section, across from the receiver battery.

My ElectroStreak uses a JoMar on-off switch for motor control. The kit includes a plastic prop and metal spinner.

Flying. Flying the ElectroStreak is a blast. Here's your chance to hotdog with an electric job.

You must use a seven-cell battery pack in the ElectroStreak; it needs the extra speed. I've had good success with 1200 MAh car packs, but I can rely on the 1800 MAh packs from SR Batteries for at least two more minutes of flight time.

The ailerons are very effective, so you don't need much throw. I have both aileron pushrods in the inner holes of the servo arm to give them as little movement as possible. Dual rate on the aileron channel would be very helpful; you could reduce the servo movement from the transmitter and test-fly it until you get it just right.

GRAUPNER ELEKTRO-UHU

Hobby Lobby International is one of the oldest mail-order hobby companies, and they have built a fine reputation over the years. Although they carry most of the popular lines, Hobby Lobby concentrates on products that only they carry—usually kits, parts, and engines that they import. Many local hobby stores carry the fine Graupner kits that Hobby Lobby imports.

Graupner is one of the major German model airplane manufacturers. They're serious about their model airplanes in Germany. Typically, German model kits are designed for adults to build and fly. They are very complete, and if you need anything not included in the kit to complete the model, it's described in detail on the outside of the box.

Hobby Lobby and Graupner have been working together for a long time. If you have questions about or problems with a Graupner kit, a call to Jim Martin and his crew at Hobby Lobby will get you the help you need. They have an excellent supply of spare parts on hand at all times. I can heartily recommend Hobby Lobby for their service to their customers; I've experienced it myself many times.

The Elektro-UHU has been a very successful kit for Hobby Lobby. They've followed it up with several more exciting electric jobs, including the Chip, which is basically a UHU with ailerons, and the remarkable Race Rat, a pistol-hot speed job that can keep up with a .40-powered Quickie 500.

The Elektro-UHU is a great little sailplane with a wide speed range—fast for climbing and thermaling, and nice and slow for landings. It's a fun airplane!

The Elektro-UHU is a typical German kit: It has well-organized multilingual instructions with very, very thorough drawings. If you are accustomed to reading and understanding technical drawings, you'll be ahead of the game. Many times something that is confusing in the written instructions will become clear when you find the right cross-section drawing on the plans sheet. Study the drawings carefully.

Hobby Lobby tucks a tube of UHU glue into the kit for you. This is the best glue to use when attaching wooden parts to the molded plastic fuselage. I found another glue that works very well: Poly Zap from Pacer. This is a super glue especially formulated for polycarbonate plastics, such as car bodies and windshields. I wouldn't trust any glue other than these two to make a firm bond to the plastic fuselage.

Motor. Hobby Lobby recommends the Graupner Speed 600 for the Elektro-UHU. This motor

Lou Ward shows off the Elektro-UHU in the AMA Museum. Yes, she's flown it, and she likes it!

comes packaged with a wonderful scimitar-bladed folding prop, noise-reducing capacitors, wiring, and an assortment of special tools to put it all together. This package is the best way to power your Elektro-UHU; bash-fitting a different motor is more trouble than it's worth.

The folding prop is simple to assemble using the exploded drawing. The prop is held on the motor shaft by a collet that tightens when the main prop nut is tightened down. I never had a problem with this system. The only surprise was that the screws that hold the prop blades to the hub were too small for the included screwdriver!

The folding prop is worthy of special note. It folds back smoothly to the nose of the plane; they were in fact designed for each other. It's a very efficient propeller that gives you an outstanding climb; the UHU climbs with some of my hotter cobalt motor-powered jobs. And the power system is considerably less expensive than a cobalt motor.

The prop blades are unlikely to suffer damage in a landing, since they're snuggled up against the fuselage. I have managed to crack the nose cone by hitting a stone in the middle of the runway. A call to Hobby Lobby had a replacement on the way quickly. I got stubborn and made a few flights with the cracked nose cone (after *very* carefully examining the prop and making sure that there was no damage to the prop blades or hub!). But there was a noticeable drop in climbing power, and the prop made much more noise than usual. I surmised that the noise was from an out-of-balance condition, and quit flying with it. An unbalanced prop puts an unnecessary strain on the engine bearings, and can weaken the structure of the prop.

There have been rare reports of prop blades coming off this unit in flight. It seems to happen when the plane is diving at a high rate of speed and the engine is turned on. I can't think of any reason why you'd do something like this in normal flight, but if you enjoy a bit of hot-dogging you should be aware of the stresses you're putting on the prop. If the prop does throw a blade, shut the motor down *immediately* to prevent damage to the motor. You should have no problem making a normal approach and landing.

Construction. Before you begin, examine the plans carefully. Start with the exploded view of the entire airplane. I pinned this up on the wall next to my workbench. With the construction drawings in front of me, I read through the instructions, locating the drawings that are relevant to each step. When I finished, I had a clear idea of how the whole thing fits together.

The drawing has callouts in German, but the English instruction sheet has translations for all of them. You'll help familiarize yourself with construction if you take the time now to read all these notes.

Graupner's trick of numbering each part in the sequence that you'll need it for construction is a tremendous help. In fact, in a couple of cases, parts that were in sequence were left out of the written instructions. This could have caused major headaches if I hadn't studied the drawings first and realized that they had to be assembled in order.

With that understood, the average beginning model builder will have no trouble with this kit. It's not an ARF kit, in spite of the molded plastic fuselage. Be prepared to spend a few evenings getting it together; it took me four days of evening work. But it's easy work, made much easier by the outstanding way all the parts fit together.

Fuselage. The molded ''Perfekt'' fuselage is a beautiful piece of work; it is indeed perfect in every detail. No sanding along the mold line was necessary with mine. If you paint the fuselage, it should be sanded very lightly to allow better adhesion. You must use a paint that is formulated for acrylic or polycarbonate plastic; any of the popular paints for RC car bodies would work fine. I left the fuselage unpainted and applied striping tape for decoration.

The fuselage is prepared by sawing off projecting knobs on the front and the back. The hole in the front is sized to fit the front bearing of the electric motor. The hole in the rear is to clear the elevator pushrod and horn. I used a Zona saw to lop these off, trimming them to final shape with a knife and sandpaper. You'll find the plastic fuselage material is very easy to work with. Put a fresh blade in your knife, and don't try to cut all the way through in one stroke.

Things you'll need to finish the Elektro-UHU: radio system, Graupner Power Switch, Direct Drive Speed 600 motor, Tee-Bar sander, and battery pack.

The motor is held in place by two screws, with a plywood doubler to reinforce the nose. Like all the other parts, the firewall is die-cut to perfection. I sanded it very slightly along the cut edges to smooth it, and glued it in place with the cement supplied.

The instructions don't mention it, but you should cut open the cooling air inlets and exits now. Look at the picture on the box to get a good idea of how the openings should be shaped. Cut them undersize and round them out to final size with a small file or sanding dowel. Ace RC Sanding Stix are very good for this kind of work.

Don't glue the battery platform in place until you have fitted the servos. The servos should rest against the bottom of the fuselage. I had to widen the servo holes slightly to fit the two standard JR servos in the platform. Once they're in, remove them, slip the platform in through the canopy opening, reinstall the servos, press the platform into position, and run a bead of glue around the edges.

Widen the holes in piece 16 so that the outer pushrod tubes fit through them easily. Install piece 16 in the rear of the radio compartment, with the holes lining up with the servo output arms. This way the pushrods won't have to flex up or down. Get piece 16 as far back in the fuselage as you can get it, so it doesn't interfere with the movement of the clevises. Test-fit it before you glue it in. In my case, this meant that piece 16 was back by the air outlets. I got it into place by gluing a long balsa stick to it, positioning it by holding onto the stick, and gluing it through the outlet holes. Don't omit this piece; you have to have some sort of support for the pushrod tubes at this end, or they'll flex instead of moving the control surfaces.

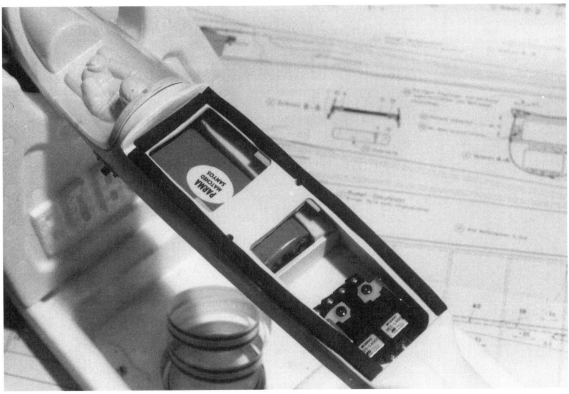

A plywood piece keeps the battery from sliding backward and changing the center of gravity. Use foam rubber at the sides to keep the pack from shifting.

Once piece 16 is in place, you can glue in the outer pushrod tubes. Glue them almost flush with piece 16. Cut the rudder pushrod tube so that it projects about two inches from the exit hole, and glue it to the hole. Cut the elevator pushrod so that it is about two inches inside the rear of the fuselage. The elevator tube must not touch the elevator clevis or it will interfere with proper control movement. It doesn't have to be supported at the rear of the fuselage.

The instructions show the wing attachment pieces that glue into the top of the fuselage as two pieces number 4. These are cut from a piece of triangle stock, and the remainder is used to attach the canopy. See the drawing F-F on the plan for the precise lengths.

Canopy. The canopy setup might seem complicated, but if you follow the instructions you'll find it goes together easily. The plastic is very easy to

work with. I trimmed the cockpit and the clear canopy to shape with scissors, being careful to cut *outside* the lines on the first cut and trimming them to the exact shape with the second cut. If you're artistically inclined, the pilot figure can be painted up easily with a fine brush. I glued the clear canopy on with Poly Zap, which grabs quickly and dries clear. It flows easily into the joint, so I got everything lined up and Scotch-taped into position before putting the glue on.

Positioning of the canopy hold-down, pieces 11 and 12, might seem tricky. It doesn't have to be precise. I glued the two wooden pieces together and then glued them to the underside of the canopy with Poly Zap. Rounding the corners of piece 12 allowed it to fit inside the openings at the forward edges of the fuselage and slide back to fit flush against the opening.

The shank screw, part 13, is intended to allow

I glued in a support at the forward end of the pushrod tubes. I stuck it to a stick with one drop of CyA, spread cement on the support, and inserted it in the rear of the fuselage.

you to snap the canopy in place. I screwed it into position on the fuselage as shown on the plans. Then I slid the canopy into position and marked it where the screw head touched it. I drilled a small hole on my mark and checked it again, then widened the hole until the screw fits into it. Backing the screw out slightly gives me a nice, positive lock when I push the canopy back. It did blow off in flight once, but that was because I only had one side of the canopy hold-down piece slid in. Incidentally, I had no problems with the airplane after the canopy departed; I circled tightly around the spot where it fell to mark it in my mind, made a normal landing, and walked right to the canopy once the plane was on the ground.

Tail Surfaces. The tail surfaces are pre-cut balsa. All of the hard shaping is done; all you have to do is line up the vertical fin and the rudder, and sand the tops to a nice smooth shape.

The horizontal stabilizer needs to have a recess cut in its trailing edge for the rear of the fuselage. Study the drawings and make the recess with a sanding tool. Then open out the slit in the fuselage at the front and the back, a little at a time, until the stabilizer will slide into place. Position it so that the trailing edge is straight, and the elevator can be hinged to it with no interference from the back of the plastic fuselage. Make two pencil marks along the edges of the fuselage on the stabilizer; this will allow you to cut away the covering for a solid glue joint.

Test-fit the vertical fin in place, making sure it fits into the slot in the stabilizer. Look at the plans and make sure that you have the fin at the right angle. Now draw light lines along the edges of the fuselage on the fin.

I covered the tail surfaces with SIG Superkote, which is very light and easy to work with. It's a low-temperature covering, and goes around corners very easily. My pencil marks showed through, so it was easy to cut away the covering where I wanted bare wood for a glue joint. The UHU cement supplied with the kit works very well for attaching the tail surfaces.

I was a little leery of the taped hinges, but they've proven to work just fine. Take your time and get them on straight. Only one side, the flat side, of the rudder is taped. Tape the upper side of the elevator first, fold it up as far as it will go, and apply the tape to the underside. There's a generous roll of hinge tape to work with, so don't worry about wasting any.

I was also a little suspicious of the control horns. Instead of bolting to the control surfaces, these horns have a projecting stud that glues into a hole drilled into the surface. The trick, I found, is to cut away the covering around the hole so the flange under the horn can make a good glue joint with the bare wood. If it's just glued to the covering, it won't hold. Again, the cement supplied works very well for this.

Before you attach the rudder horn, hook up the rudder pushrod and clevis. You'll want to attach the horn at a slight downward-facing angle so that the pushrod doesn't flex excessively as it moves in and out.

Radio Installation. Installing the radio sys-tem is simple, once the wooden radio tray is in place. I used double-sided tape to secure the receiver and power switch to the bottom of the fuselage. First, I applied the tape to the receiver, leaving the protective backing on the outside of the tape. Then I connected the leads from the servos and power switch, and slid the receiver into position. Once I had everything where I wanted it, I moved the receiver out until I could peel the backing off the tape and put it in its final position.

The power switch can go in the same way. Be sure that the battery connector is facing forward, so there will be plenty of slack to make it easier for you to connect the drive battery pack.

Pushrods. The nylon pushrods supplied are very flexible and smooth. As long as they are well-supported, they'll work fine. Clevises are perma-nently attached to one end. Screw these halfway out, so you can adjust them both ways when you install them.

The pushrods need to be cut to length on the outer end. When you cut them, shape the cut end to a point to make it easier to thread the clevis on.

Two nylon bolts hold the wing panels in place. This is much neater and more convenient than rubber bands.

The Elektro-UHU uses Graupner's remarkable scimitar-blade folding prop. This unit is good for most standard direct-drive systems. Several sizes are available.

Center your servos first by turning on your radio system and making sure your rudder and elevator trim switches are in the center. Run the pushrods through the outer tubes and attach the clevises to the servo arms. Now attach a clevis to the rudder horn. Measure and cut the rudder pushrod so that the clevis can be threaded all the way onto it; you want to have as much of the pushrod threaded into the clevis as possible. Now remove the clevis from the horn and carefully thread it onto the rod. It helps to hold the pushrod with a pair of pliers. Don't twist too hard, or you might break off a piece of the pushrod inside the clevis. If it's going on very hard, back it off and try again.

Measuring the elevator pushrod is trickier, since the clevis is inside the rear of the fuselage.

Use the same method you used for the rudder pushrod. The most important thing here is to make sure the clevis doesn't hit the outer pushrod tube when you give it full down elevator.

Radio. I used a JR Max four-channel system for the Elektro-UHU. This is a very good system at a very low price.

Graupner makes a special power switch for electric flight. It's strongly recommended for the Elektro-UHU. Now that I've had a chance to test it, I recommend it for just about any electric airplane that uses seven cells or less for power. It's great!

The power switch gives you on-off control. It also has circuitry to continually measure the voltage of the battery pack. When the pack is discharged to a pre-set level, the power switch shuts off the motor and won't let you turn it back on. This is because it's also powering the receiver from the drive battery pack. When the circuit cuts off, you have adequate power for about 10 minutes of running the receiver. The beauty of this system is that you don't have to carry another battery just for the receiver. Not only does it save you a few ounces of weight, but it's one less battery you have to charge before you can go flying!

I was a little leery of this system at first. After all, ni-cd batteries will rebound to a higher voltage when the load is taken away. What if you were coming in for a landing and tried to turn the motor back on? Would the load of the motor drag down the battery voltage to the point where you'd lose control of the receiver? And just how much time do you have

left on the receiver when the circuit shuts off the motor?

I devised a test. I soldered a 500 milliamp resistor to a servo connector. I ran the motor on my workbench until the power switch shut it off. Then I plugged my resistor into the receiver and wiggled the servos until the battery pack could no longer power the receiver. It ran for eight minutes.

That 500 milliamp resistor is more load than the battery should ever see from a servo. A servo will draw that much current if it is stalled, trying to move against an obstruction of some sort. This won't happen on a plane like the Elektro-UHU unless you have dramatically fouled up your pushrod installation, so I considered this a good worst-case test. After many flights, I've never had reason to

The Elektro-UHU's elevator control horn is almost hidden in the rear of the fuselage. Connect the clevis before you glue the horn to the elevator.

doubt that the power switch was doing its job.

Wing Construction. The wing is the part you'll spend the most time building. It's time well spent. Everything goes together beautifully; I've seldom seen such good die-cutting in a model kit. The good fit will encourage you to do a little more sanding and make it look perfect.

The instructions mention part 33, which is part of the bottom wing sheeting, but not part 34, which goes on right next to it. Put them both on at the same time, dry-fitting them before gluing.

The wing tapers toward the tip, so all the ribs are a different size. Once you have the bottom sheeting and spar down, all you have to do is glue a rib, a spar web, and the next rib all the way out to the end. It's fun.

The top sheeting can be a bit tricky; study the drawing. Let part 66 lap over the root rib and leading edge, and align its back surface with the spar. Glue part 66 down, then part 67, then part 65, then part 33, checking each part's fit and sanding it if necessary.

I used a flat Tee-Bar sander to get the wing nice and smooth. Pay careful attention to the joint at the front and back of each rib; projecting knobs of glue will look terrible when the wing is covered! When I was through, I was so pleased that I covered the wing panels with transparent orange Supercoat film. It looks great. It would look a little better if I had remembered to sand the printed numbers off the ribs, but I can't do *everything* right!

You should test-join the wing panels before covering them. I got tired of trying to keep the metal wing brace in position in one panel while putting the other panel in place, and finally super-glued it into one panel. Now it doesn't move, and I won't lose it either. A little sanding with a Wedge Lock sanding block was necessary to get a good fit all the way along the inner surfaces of the wing panels.

When you drill the holes for the wing bolts, you'll make your life a lot easier if you have a good cradle to hold the fuselage. I used a Robart Super Stand with cloth sandbags holding the fuselage straight and true. I put foam wing seating tape on the top of the fuselage wing saddle to keep the wing from slipping. I propped up the wing on the fuse-lage, looked at it from all sides, and drilled a pilot hole in one wing panel. You guessed it—it was a little too far out, and I poked the drill through the side of the fuselage. Another small hole right next to it was where it belonged. I reamed out the good hole, glued the nut into the fuselage, and screwed the wing panel into place before drilling the second hole. This one came out right the first time.

After a few choice words, I attacked the hole in the side of the fuselage with some fine sandpaper. After cleaning it up, I discovered that Model Magic Filler sticks to the plastic fuselage just fine. You can hardly see the hole now. Phew!

Flying. Now for the fun part! The UHU wings and fuselage make a compact package, easily stowed in the back seat of any compact car. I keep the nylon wing bolts screwed into the fuselage so I don't lose them. When I attach the wing, I join the two panels, insert the screws into the holes in the wings, and poke the screws into the holes in the wing saddle. A small screwdriver is all I need to snug them down. I sight down the front of the plane once or twice as I tighten them to be sure the wing isn't farther down on one side or the other.

The battery is easily accessible behind the canopy. I fly with three battery packs: one to fly, one to charge, and one to cool down. This is good for hours of continuous flying and charging. In fact, I've had one merry afternoon session of flying the UHU where I charged the batteries so many times that I couldn't get my car started! So much for Die Hard batteries.

Switch on your transmitter before you connect the battery to the power switch, just in case the receiver switch was left on. Glance at your throttle stick to make sure it's in the off position. Now plug in the battery, fit the canopy in place, and switch on the receiver. Wiggle the tail surfaces just to make sure everything's okay. Now face into the wind, hold the UHU high, switch on the motor, and give it a firm shove straight into the wind. Don't do a jave-lin-throw with the nose pointing up; you could throw the plane into a stall.

I've always launched my UHU from a standing start. It starts to climb immediately, and I have plenty of time to get my transmitter into my right

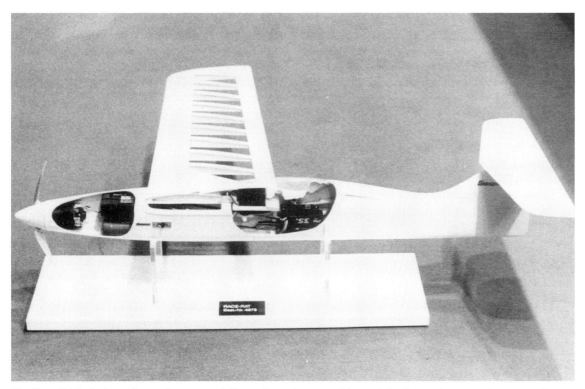

The Race Rat is designed for maximum speed. Three channels are used for control: aileron, elevator, and motor on-off.

hand and my thumbs on the sticks. You can feel how steep an angle of climb you can hold; if the plane starts to "mush" or drop its nose, back off the up elevator. It takes me a minute or so to get up to thermal altitude. When I shut down the motor I generally trim in a couple of clicks of up to settle into a good glide attitude. Then I just relax and enjoy it. A lawn chair is an essential piece of field equipment for UHU flying.

The Elektro-UHU will turn as tightly as you want; establish a bank angle with rudder and add up elevator to tighten the turn. Opposite rudder will flatten the turn and let you take advantage of a thermal. This plane is fast and responsive, just as sweet as you please in any flight regieme.

Landing approaches should be made from some distance out, since the power-off glide is very flat. You may find it necessary to give a tiny bit of down elevator to get it to land.

I have had excellent results with six-cell 1200 MAh battery packs and seven-cell 800 MAh packs. These packs are approximately the same size. When I decided to try a seven-cell pack of SR's 1800 MAh cells (which are sub-C size like "standard" 1200 MAh cells) I found that I had to move the ply piece under the wings back to make room. No problem. Then the next time I tried to fly with a six-cell pack, the pack was a very loose fit. I stuffed a piece of foam in next to it to hold it in place—not a smart move. When I launched it, the pack slid all the way back, pulling the plane up into a full stall. I tried to get the nose down, but ran out of altitude and shut off the motor to minimize the damage. The UHU hit on the nose and the right wingtip. The only damage was snapping one of the nylon wing bolts. Relief! I found that the bolts are metric, so I had to order another set from Hobby Lobby.

If you're a beginner, set up the controls so that the rudder and elevator move the distances shown on the plan, no farther. The UHU can tolerate more control throw, but it can give an inexperienced pilot grief, too. I got caught this way once on a hot approach, when I decided the UHU was coming in too fast and pulled up for a go-around. I made the mistake of turning on the motor when the UHU was in a tight right turn, and torque-rolled it into the ground. This time the only damage was a broken prop blade.

The Elektro-UHU is one of the finest planes I've ever flown. I strongly recommend it for your first electric job, especially if you enjoy sailplanes. Set up with the control throws shown on the plans, and it's a forgiving trainer with a very flat glide. Add more throw and it has all the performance you'd want.

HOBBY SHACK EZ ELEC.1800

EZ kits were among the first ready-built airplanes available, and they are very sophisticated.

Construction of EZ kits is unique. Fuselages and wings are made from a balsa and light ply skeleton. A layer of Styrofoam board about $3/8''$ thick is laminated around the skeleton, with plastic joiners at the seams. A printed wrap gives you the colors of the airplane, and a clear overwrap fuelproofs the whole business. Elevators, stabilizers, rudders, and fins are usually laminated foam board with the color overlays and formed plastic pieces on the tips to seal them. All hinges are in place and ready to be glued in.

This gives you a beautifully finished airframe with a solid structure to mount your engine and radio. It's also surprisingly durable. A hard landing that doesn't break the underlying structure will, at worst, crease the foam a bit. One disadvantage of this construction is that major repairs are difficult; it's much easier to just replace major components.

Construction. All EZ kits come with well-

The EZ Elec. 1800 is a large, sleek sailplane with a geared motor and folding prop. I used the JR Max radio, which is an excellent sport-priced system.

The gear drive in the Elec.1800 must be carefully assembled. A bronze bushing holds the shaft extension straight.

illustrated instruction manuals. You'll need some five-minute epoxy. You can also use Poly Zap, a special formulation of CyA glue that doesn't destroy foam plastic. I used Poly Zap throughout the Elec.1800; it bonds quickly and tightly.

Don't mount the tail on the fuselage until you have the wing ready for mounting. Attach the wing, spread epoxy on the tail, put it in the slot, and use the wing to make it easier to eyeball the tail straight.

The fuselage is a tight fit! Do what they tell you in the order that they tell you and you'll have no problems. Don't rush it.

I couldn't make a seven-cell pack and the connectors fit into the fuselage comfortably. Six cells turned out to provide more than enough power.

Motor and Gear Unit. Assembling the motor

and gear drive can be tricky. The blue aluminum piece with the two big holes closer together is the rear piece. I used PIC Vibra-Jam on all the screws—just a tiny drop on the threads. This keeps them from loosening and throwing the gears out of alignment.

The instructions recommend that you widen the two holes in the rear plate that accept the bolts to attach the plate to the motor, to allow you to adjust the gear mesh. In my opinion, this is more than just a recommendation, it's *crucial*. I tried it the first time without taking the trouble to modify the holes, and chewed the teeth off the pinion gear after three flights.

My prop blades fit perfectly in the aluminum hub with no modification. Tightening the main bolt that holds the hub in place was a bit tricky; I inserted the Allen wrench in the prop shaft set screw and used it to keep the prop shaft from turning. Screw in the main bolt until it's finger-tight, then test fit the spinner nose cone on the backplate. You might have to rotate the prop hub until the spinner fits all the way in. Once it fits, tighten the main bolt with the supplied Allen wrench.

Pushrods. The kit includes a tree with lots of extra plastic parts! Use the illustrations to figure out which ones you need.

Install a long rod in one inner pushrod tube and put a clevis on it. Run the other end of the pushrod into the outer tube from the back. Do the same with the other pushrod. Now get a control horn from the tree. Attach it to the clevis on the elevator side, and position it as shown on the plans. Use a drop of Poly Zap to hold it in place on the elevator. Remove the clevis, drill the holes, and attach the horn permanently. Hook the clevis to it again.

Now look at the other end of the pushrod.

Attach a clevis to a short threaded rod, and use it to measure how much of the pushrod needs to be cut off. Leave yourself at least a quarter of an inch of pushrod to thread the rod into. Cut off the pushrod, attach the rod and clevis, and clip the clevis to the servo horn; it's much easier to do if you remove the horn from the servo first.

Turn on your transmitter and receiver, and check to be sure that the throttle trim is centered. Now put the servo horn, with clevis attached, back on the servo. Check elevator movement. If the elevator isn't neutral when the elevator stick is centered, adjust it by screwing the clevis that connects to the elevator horn in or out.

You can use the same procedure to hook up the rudder, with one exception. The bolts that attach the horn to the rudder have to run through short pieces of copper tubing. This keeps the horn plates from crushing the rudder, which is just a sheet of laminated foam.

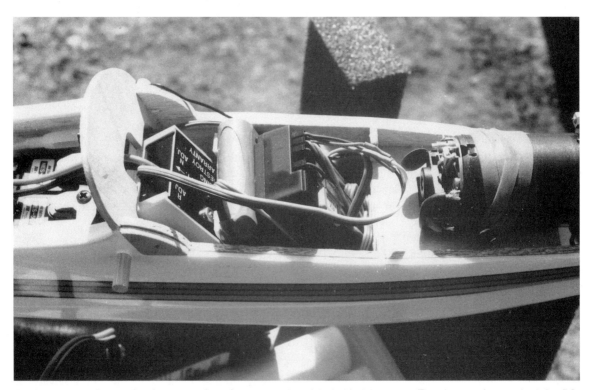

The speed controller, receiver battery, and receiver are stacked right behind the motor. There's room for standard-size RC equipment.

Radio and Speed Control. I used the new JR Max four-channel system from Hobby Dynamics; it's available at most hobby stores. This is an economical system, but still has some very nice features in spite of the low price. All four channels have servo reversing, of course. I particularly like the transmitter, which is nicely balanced and shaped to fit your hands on the sides.

The speed controller you select must have a brake. I found this out the hard way when I clipped off a prop blade on landing. The plane was moving pretty fast when I shut the motor off, and the windmill effect kept the prop spinning until I touched down. A brake would have stopped the prop and saved that blade. Rather than replace the Robart speed controller that I had installed, I added a JoMar brake unit. This is a tiny little circuit board that connects to the motor leads. It mounted easily

There's just enough room in the slim Elec. 1800 fuselage for two standard servos and a six-cell battery pack.

on top of the speed controller with double-sided tape. When you shut off the motor, the JoMar unit stops the prop solidly, allowing it to fold the blades back out of harm's way.

Flying. The Elec.1800 flies like a high-performance sailplane. As I mentioned, I was a bit surprised by the clashing noise coming out of the gear drive, but it pulled the plane right up to altitude smartly. When I shut the motor down, a few clicks of up trim were necessary to put the plane into glide trim.

On the third flight I got a sudden increase in noise during the second climb. I shut the motor down and brought the plane home. The two brass gears had started to eat each others' teeth off. I ordered a new set of gears from Hobby Shack, and when they came I rechecked the alignment of the whole gear drive unit before tightening it all down. These gears make much less noise than the originals.

Hobby Shack will soon be releasing a new electric glider called the LOTA 1700E. It will feature a direct-drive motor with scimitar-bladed folding prop. All construction is done the same as other EZ kits. The fuselage is blow-molded plastic, which is considerably stronger than the fuselage on the Elec.1800. It looks like a winner!

KYOSHO CESSNA CARDINAL

Kyosho has been making almost-ready-to-fly electric models for a few years, and I've had the chance to fly several of them. They all have molded plastic fuselages (which are tough but somewhat heavy) and beautifully-built pre-covered wings.

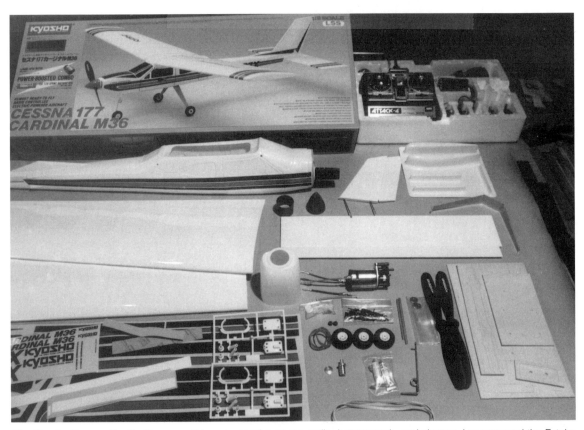

The Kyosho Cessna Cardinal has everything you need except a radio, battery pack, and charger. I recommend the Futaba Attack MCR-4A radio system.

The Cardinal battery pack is held in place by four plastic clips. Six-cell 1200 MAh packs and seven-cell 800 MAh packs will fit. Remove the wing to change packs.

In my opinion, the Cessna Cardinal is the best of the Kyosho electrics. Kyosho's Zero and Robin are almost unflyable unless you're an expert. The Valencia is a nice little plane, but suffers from sloppy control linkages; besides, low-wing planes are notoriously difficult to hand-launch. The Cardinal has none of these faults. It's simple, it's easy to assemble, and it flies very well indeed.

Assembly. The Kyosho Cardinal has a molded fuselage that is very easy to work with. The first thing to do is to install the ply plate that reinforces the main landing gear. The non-steerable nose gear bolts in underneath the cowl.

Install the pushrods before you put the radio mounting plate in place.

Since the plastic fuselage is fairly heavy to start with, I decided to use a lightweight radio system. Kyosho sells a cutoff unit that gives you on-off control from the transmitter's throttle stick, and powers the receiver from the drive battery pack. This (or a similar system, such as the Graupner Power Switch or the Futaba MCR-4A system) is the only way to go, in my opinion. I used Futaba's sailplane system, with micro receiver and servos. Since the cutouts in the radio plate are made for standard size servos, I made an adapter plate with a

The tail of the Kyosho Cardinal is built and covered. The vertical fin has two bolts on the bottom that hold the stabilizer in place.

section of one of the punched-out pieces. It's a simple installation with no challenges.

Once you have the fuselage assembled, you can fit the wing. Kyosho has done all of the hard work for you. The wing is already built-up and covered, and the construction is excellent. All you have to do is epoxy the two halves together and install the molded plastic wingtips. I glued the tips on with Super Jet.

When the wing halves are joined, you have to cut a piece out of the trailing edge in the center so that it fits down onto the fuselage. Measure it by fitting the leading edge into the wing saddle and marking where the sides touch the rear of the wing.

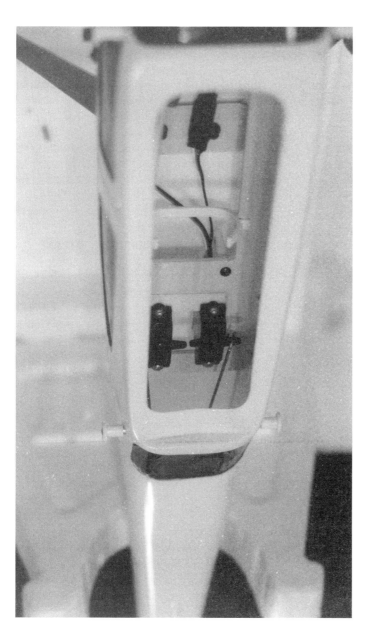

The Cardinal's fuselage is a one-piece plastic molding. The wood radio tray bolts in. Micro servos require a wood spacer.

When you have the wing fitting properly, wrap the center section with the supplied white plastic tape.

The tail section is already built. Two rods project from the bottom of the vertical fin. They fit down into two holes in the top of the fuselage, through the stabilizer, and out the bottom of the fuselage. Two plastic caps thread onto the rods to hold the whole assembly in place. It couldn't be simpler.

Flying. The Cardinal is set up to use interchangable battery packs, but you have to take the wing off to get at the battery. Use at least four rubber bands—two on each side—to attach the wing. As always, I prefer to fly the Cardinal with a seven-cell battery; the climb is better. But it flies just fine on six 1200 MAh cells.

Hand-launches are simple, and the Cardinal's gentle flying will make it easy for you. The wheels are too small to try taking off from grass. On pavement, the Cardinal tracks straight and has plenty of power to rise off the ground.

The Kyosho Cardinal is a very good choice for an almost-ready-to-fly trainer plane. It'll get you in

the air quickly, and is gentle enough to train you without scaring you.

LEISURE ELECTRONICS AMPTIQUE

Leisure Electronics has been in the electric flight business for a long time. They have some of the best kits you can get. Leisure's Senior Playboy helped start the electric revolution; it was one of the first electric-powered planes with truly spectacular performance. Based on a very popular free-flight kit from the 1940s, the Playboy is incredibly stable. Its undercambered wing and stick-type fuselage make it an intimidating building project for the rank beginner, however.

A better choice for your first RC electric is the Amptique, which has been a standard electric-powered trainer for many years. Its delightful flying characteristics are the main reason for its popularity. Anyone who can see far enough can fly an Amptique.

This plane is designed around the Leisure LT50 gear drive power system, and the firewall has pre-drilled mounting holes for it. I suppose you

Leisure Electronics' Senior Playboy was one of the first successful electric kits, and it's still one of the finest fliers around. I've never seen anything fly so slowly!

could fit another motor in it, but there's no earthly reason to take the trouble. The LT50 is relatively inexpensive, easy to use, and readily available. If you crash it and break a tooth off one of the gears, replacements are plentiful and easy to install. The ferrite magnet motor gets a good long motor run with any common battery pack. Why change it?

Construction. The Amptique is a conventional model airplane; there's nothing almost-ready-to-fly about it. The wood in the kit is of a very high grade, and there's no die-cutting; all parts are sawn or sanded to shape for you. Even the ribs are stack-sanded. This is a high-quality kit that you'll enjoy building.

The instructions are a bit skimpy, especially as compared to the AeroLectric or PT-Electric. This won't bother you if it's not your first RC airplane, but we'll assume that it is, and look at some of the parts that you might find confusing.

First of all are the fuselage sides. They are pre-

The author launches his Leisure Playboy. The undercambered wing is not easy to build and cover, but the performance is fabulous.

cut sheet balsa, reinforced by gluing $^1/_{16}''$ square balsa sticks to the insides. If you pin the side down to the plan, you can't see where to put the sticks any more. Make some pencil marks on the plans to guide you. Note that the plywood firewall (I guess it's more of an engine mounting plate than a firewall) glues on the *inside* of the sheet sides, with sticks right behind it to reinforce it. Use the firewall as a guide to glue the sticks in place for right now.

Building with sticks is really easy; I enjoy it. Using a razor saw, I measure each stick against the plan and cut it slightly long. Then I sand the cut end a tiny bit until it's a perfect fit. If the stick fits in at an angle you can eyeball the angle, or you can use a slick little gadget called a Miter Master. This is a frame with a sliding sanding block and an adjustable gauge to hold your piece at the right angle. It makes precise fitting of angled sticks quick and painless.

Measure and cut to length the top and bottom crosspieces before you join the fuselage sides. The best way to join the sides is over the plans, and you don't want to move the assembly every time you have to cut a stick. Use pliers to put the bottom crosspieces in while the sides are still pinned to the plans.

The vertical pieces on the right and left sides of the firewall will have to be sanded slightly to let the motor through.

Battery Hatch. The Amptique is set up so that you have to remove the wing to get at the battery pack. I decided to rig up a hatch so I could get at the batteries from the underside of the fuselage. A seven-cell 800 MAh flat battery pack will fit nicely on the fuselage floor. The Leisure LT-50 gear drive motor can be bought with a seven-cell pack, but it's in an unusual configuration—the batteries are stacked in a pyramid. This also works well with a removable hatch.

I made a tongue out of a piece of scrap ply that holds the forward end of the hatch in place on the fuselage. Then I made two small ply reinforcement plates and glued one to the rear of the hatch, the other inside the fuselage bottom close to the edge of the hatch hole. Then I installed a Goldberg hatch hold-down on the underside of the fuselage. This little nylon part is held in place by a screw that

threads into the ply plate into the fuselage. It swings around and clips onto another screw that threads into the ply plate on the hatch. A couple of Velcro patches on the inside of the hatch keep the pack from sliding around.

Radio System. Any radio system will fit the Amptique nicely; there's room in the fuselage for standard size servos. Mini servos will be easier to install and save you some weight. As usual, a system such as the Futaba MCR-4A, Kyosho Auto Cutoff unit, or Graupner Power Switch will be very good. If you use a speed controller or servo-operated micro switch, the Airtronics Vanguard with mini servos, Ace Oly 5 with mini servos, or JR Max would be good bets. I used the Ace Oly 5 with Silver Seven receiver, two mini servos, and a micro servo with a microswitch for motor on-off control.

A speed controller to give you proportional control of the motor from the throttle stick is a good idea with the Amptique. It lets you set the motor for cruise speed, a point where you can easily maintain altitude but are not draining the batteries at full speed. If you use a car controller, remember to use a separate battery pack for the receiver even if the controller has a battery eliminator circuit. A very small pack will do, since the receiver will only draw on it when the drive battery voltage is too low to power the receiver.

Flying. The Amptique is a slow, gentle flier that a beginner can enjoy the first time out. The Leisure gear drive unit is one of the best powerplants available for electric jobs, and when it's combined with a well-designed plane, the result is delightful.

Hand-launches are best for the Amptique, since there isn't that much clearance between the prop and the ground. You can try taking off from hard-surfaced runways after you get accustomed to the plane, but be sure to avoid nosing over and hitting the prop on the ground. This can break teeth or bend the shaft in the gear drive. If you *do* manage to damage the drive, parts are easily replaceable.

If your Amptique has on-off motor control, you can use it to get up to altitude in about a minute. Then you can shut off and enjoy the Amptique's

The Amptique fuselage is built from sheet sides and connected with stringers. The firewall is pre-drilled for the Leisure gear drive unit.

excellent glide. But, as I said earlier, the best way to fly this plane is with a proportional speed control. Bore up to altitude at full throttle, then knock the stick back to about half throttle. Trim the elevator to keep the nose level. Once you've cruised around at this setting for a bit, bring the throttle back another click or two. See if the nose starts to drop. If it drops slightly, add up elevator trim to level it out. This is the point where you can cruise around the sky for seven or eight minutes, without touching the throttle. If you get in trouble, hit the throttle and the elevator trim you've added will help take you back upstairs.

When you can hear the motor slow down, or when you advance the throttle and don't get any more speed, it's time to land. Shut off the engine and set up your approach. Because of the up elevator trim, the Amptique may try to float off the end of the runway, so add a little down elevator to stick

the wheels onto the ground until the plane slows down.

The Amptique isn't the simplest plane for a beginner to build, but its sweet flying performance more than pays you back for the extra effort.

MIDWEST AEROLECTRIC

The AeroLectric is an electric version of Midwest's popular AeroStar series, joining the Aero-Star 20 and AeroStar 40 gas models. These models are easily recognizable by their long, sloping windshields and stabilizers mounted on the bottom of the fuselage. All three of these kits are also distinguished by their beautifully detailed "Success Series" instruction books, parts in numbered bags, and outstanding parts cut and fit. The self-adhesive decals are even pre-cut for you. You can select any one of these planes for your first RC job and be sure you'll get a pleasant building experience. You'll

Midwest Products has three primary trainers in their AeroStar series: the AeroStar .20, the AeroStar .40, and the AeroLectric. All are excellent kits for your first RC model.

learn a lot, too. There's no better way to get started.

The success of the AeroLectric has led Midwest to design an electric version of their "Hots" aerobatic job. The Electric Hots is every bit as easy to build as the AeroLectric, and is a remarkable performer. It'll do every maneuver in the book, and thanks to its relatively thick airfoil, behaves itself better than most aerobatic planes with the power off for landing.

To get decent flying performance, an electric model must have a light airframe. The rule-of-thumb is that the power system (motor and battery) should be no more than 50 percent of the weight of the plane for ideal performance. Achieving this goal

is a real challenge to kit designers, who have to produce a model that performs well but isn't too expensive to put in the box.

Midwest Products has taken an interesting approach with the AeroLectric. Unlike some kits, which achieve lightness by cutting holes in all the substantial wood parts, there are no holes in the AeroLectric. Other kits use special design techniques, such as having fewer ribs in a wing panel or building the tail surfaces from sticks, but the AeroLectric is a basic, simple, conventional design with sheet sides and tail. The AeroLectric's secret is in the wood. All of the wood for each component is carefully selected and graded, so no part is heavier than it has to be. Since Midwest Products is one of

The author gets ready to launch his AeroLectric. This is one of my favorite planes—very easy to build and a very enjoyable flier.

the largest processors of balsa wood in the world, it's no surprise that their expertise in wood selection should show up in their kits. It sure pays off in the AeroLectric, giving you a simple, sturdy airplane with sparkling performance.

The AeroLectric kit is complete, in the truest sense of the word. Wheels, all hardware, prop, and spinner are right in the box. The only things you'll need are a radio system, two rolls of covering material, and a battery pack and charger.

I selected the Futaba MCR-4A radio system for my AeroLectric. Using this system, which has a proportional speed control and a battery eliminator circuit in the receiver as well as micro size servos,

saved me six ounces of weight right at the start. The AeroLectric power system comes with a switch harness and hardware to set up on-off control with a standard servo, so any modern RC system will work very well. I wanted the proportional speed control so I could experiment with finding a cruise speed that would give me a longer battery run. (More on this later.) If you do go with a standard radio system, I recommend getting a 200 MAh battery pack for the receiver; you'll save nearly two ounces.

The AeroLectric is very easy to cover, since it doesn't have any fancy curves, so any common covering will work fine. I like Super Coverite, which is

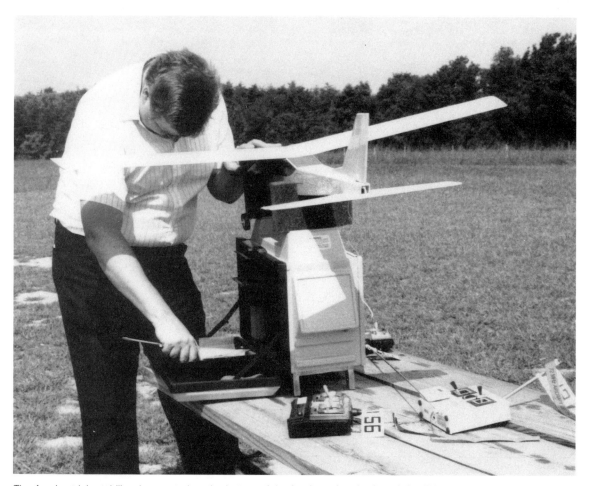

The AeroLectric's stabilizer is mounted on the bottom of the fuselage. In a bad crash it will break away cleanly rather than tearing up the rear of the fuselage.

a cloth and goes on very easily.

Construction. The numbered and bagged parts and the detailed instruction book make construction remarkably easy. You are even told which kinds of glue to use on each step.

The parts themselves are remarkable. Die-cutting is clean; I used a Mini Sander to clean up the die-cut edges of some of the ply pieces. It wasn't necessary on the balsa pieces. The wing ribs are cut and stack-sanded to perfection. Even the wing sheeting pieces are cut to the right length!

I got a lot of pleasure out of building the Aero-Lectric. I appreciate good wood, and this is the best. Everything went together so well, it took very little sanding to make the structures perfect. This is one of the few airplanes I've built where the wing halves mated perfectly with no sanding!

One thing that I would change is the design of the battery compartment. As it is, in order to change batteries, you need to remove the wing, and the nosewheel pushrod is in the way. I would have set up the nosewheel so that it doesn't steer (there's much need to taxi an electric plane). Then I would have figured out some sort of system where the battery could be removed through a hatch in the underside. Perhaps a box could be built on the battery floor, open at the front, and with Velcro at the back. The pack would slide in through the forward

Midwest's new aerobatic Electric kit, the Electric Hots, is a real performer! The thick wing gives you complete aerobatic capability and still lets you slow down for easy landings.

hatch that's already there, and Velcro on the back of the pack would hold it in place. I'll try that in a while; right now I'm having too much fun flying the fool thing to try any modifications.

When I mounted the motor to the firewall I thought that the mounting bolts went in pretty far. I spun the motor shaft by hand, and sure enough, the bolts were hitting the motor's armature. Three flat washers between the bolt head and the firewall on each side solved the problem.

As mentioned, the AeroLectric kit includes wheels and a spinner. The wheels are the super-light Dave Brown models. The spinner is a snap-on type. I found that it was necessary to support the spinner backplate while I pushed the nose cone on to keep from flexing the motor mount. A long screwdriver between the spinner backplate and fuselage front gave me something to push against.

Flying. I decided to make my first flight with a seven-cell pack to get the best possible climb. That way, I'd have the best chance of getting away from the trees around my flying site. It would also give me the best chance to recover from any odd trim conditions.

I needn't have worried. The AeroLectric climbed out beautifully from my hand-launch, solid and true, with only two clicks of down elevator trim needed to bring it out level at full power.

Turns are delightful. On the first flight I found that the plane was quite sensitive to the controls, requiring very small stick movements to make the turns. I moved the clevises to the outer holes on the control horns to reduce the control throws. It is still very responsive; I'm sure I could move the pushrod connectors to the innermost holes on the servo arms and still have a very flyable airplane. In fact, I wish my transmitter had dual rates so I could reduce the control surface travel from the transmitter. But as it is, the AeroLectric is gentle enough for any beginner. When you do your radio installation, try to get the control throws specified in the instructions; if your controls move too far, you'll have to be very gentle on the stick to keep from booting the plane all over the sky.

When I flew the AeroLectric in a wind, I was prepared for the worst, since light planes usually bounce all over in a breeze. As it turns out, the AeroLectric penetrates into the wind very well, even with the engine off. A little down elevator trim was all it took to make a very nice landing into the wind. It was a gusty breeze, too, and other planes were jumping around on final approach.

If you get yourself in trouble, remember Rule 1: The plane knows how to fly better than you do! Let the stick go back to center, and the AeroLectric will pull out of a spiral dive and give you a chance to get yourself oriented. The plane glides beautifully. When you feel it slowing down, set up your landing approach, kill the motor, and just keep it level as it settles onto the runway. The AeroLectric will make you look good every time.

POLK JUICER

Polk's Hobbies has been in the business a long time. Nowadays they specialize in imported items, and they have several that are of interest to electric fliers. Their Peak Detector Chargers are very good units. The smaller one works on six- and seven-cell packs, and is one of the best chargers you can buy for the money. The larger version will charge packs of up to eight cells at varying rates, and includes a discharge efficiency testing circuit.

Juicer. One of the newest ARF electrics to come from Polk is the Juicer. It's a conventional high-wing airplane, made of wood rather than foam, and covered with a printed film material that makes any finishing unnecessary. The Juicer includes a motor, a switch harness, and a very nice folding prop. It even includes wheels. The only things you need to fly this plane are a radio system, a battery pack, and a charger.

The instructions are skimpy, as is often the case with model kits imported from Asian manufacturers. Fortunately, the illustrations give you enough information to assemble this very simple kit.

Motor Mounting. The motor mount is a molded plastic piece. Mine was tight, so that the motor had to be forced down into it to stay at the right angle. I used a nylon tie wrap to make sure the motor stayed in. It's also helpful to fit the motor to the mount before you screw the mount to the

Jeff Troy about to hand-launch the Juicer. It has more than enough power to rise out of your hand after a few steps. Point it into the wind, and release it with the wings level.

firewall, to allow the mount to flex as the motor is inserted.

Be sure that you solder the switch harness to the motor before you mount it; the red wire goes to the motor terminal with a red dot beside it. No capacitors are supplied to reduce motor noise. You should install three capacitors before mounting the motor, one big one across the motor terminals and one each between each terminal and the motor case. BoLink sells a very nice kit containing all of these capacitors in the right sizes; your dealer should have them. If you're using an opto-isolated

speed controller such as the JoMar controllers or the Robart unit I used in the Juicer, the capacitors are unnecessary.

Radio Installation. The radio tray in the Juicer is cut out for mini (not micro) servos. I used a Futaba sailplane system with micro servos; they were a little too small for the holes, so I glued a small strip of ply to one side of each hole for the servo mounting screws.

The wooden pushrods are easy to assemble, and are the correct length. Cut slots for each push-rod to exit the fuselage where they are shown in the instructions. Then, measuring against the fuselage, bend the pushrod wires at a right angle to exit the center of the hole, and back again toward the rear. I found that I had to clip a little off the threaded end of each pushrod. You could accomplish the same thing more easily by using Du-Bro or Hobby Lobby pushrod connectors on the servo ends of the push-rods.

I mounted the receiver, receiver battery, and speed controller on the radio tray with BoLink double-sided servo tape, which is thinner and grabs better than other brands.

I used a 250 MAh pack for the receiver. This is more than enough capacity for an afternoon's flying, and saves weight and space. You can buy these smaller packs from several different sources: Ace RC, SR Batteries, or any of the radio manufacturers. Your hobby shop will probably have them,

along with the connectors you'll need to fit the pack to your receiver.

Flying. As I did with the other planes reviewed for this book, I prepared the Juicer for flight strictly in accordance with the instructions. I never thought to check the wing for warps—bad move!

That first flying session was a disaster. On the first hand-launch, I threw the Juicer so hard the drive battery shifted backwards almost an inch, making the plane tail-heavy. I had presence of mind enough to give it full down elevator, avoiding a stall and snap roll, but as soon as I released the elevator it stalled. Fortunately, it was only a few feet in the air at the time. The only damage was a wrinkle in the plastic cowl.

On the second try I got into the air without shifting the center of gravity. The Juicer flew, but it

The Juicer is completely built at the factory. Glue the wing halves, mount the motor and cowl, glue in the tail surfaces, mount the landing gear, install the radio, and it's ready.

The Juicer fuselage is built from wood. I taped the receiver and battery to the sides, leaving room for the speed controller in the forward end of the radio compartment.

would only turn to the left, and I had to put in full right trim to make it fly straight. I wrestled it back to the ground and took a look at the wing. The left wing panel was twisted up and the right panel twisted down. That'll do it, all right!

Back at the shop, I twisted the right wing panel up and used a heat gun to shrink the covering and hold the twist in place. It worked very well; in fact, it looked as though none of the covering on the wing had been shrunk at all! While I was at it, I shrank the covering over the entire wing. It looks a lot better, and now both wing panels have a little bit of washout (the trailing edges are twisted up at the tips). I also increased the rudder throw by moving the clevis to the innermost hole on the rudder horn, just in case.

The next flying session was an entirely different experience! The Juicer flew beautifully, rising right out of my hand. It cruised nicely at half throttle, giving satisfying six-minute flights on my seven-cell SR packs. On the second flight I moved the rudder clevis out one hole on the horn, since it

didn't need as much rudder throw as I thought it might.

Since the battery pack can slide through holes in the formers at the front and rear of the battery compartment, you should always make sure it's tightly strapped in before you fly. It's a good policy to check the center of gravity each time you install the battery, too. Hold the plane up with the tips of your fingers resting on the wing spars, on either side of the fuselage. If the tail is low, slide the pack forward and tighten the hold-down strap. You want the plane to balance level or a little bit nose-down. This exercise will help you avoid unpleasant surprises.

All in all, the Juicer is a very satisfying little plane. It assembles quickly and flies nicely. Watch that wing, though; check it for twists and shrink the covering before you fly it.

If you don't have a heat gun to shrink the covering, a hair dryer will work. Don't use an iron unless you absolutely have to, since it may smear the printing on the wing covering.

ROYAL PRODUCTS ELECTROSOAR

Royal Products is a model distributor and importer that has been in the business a long time. As this was being written, they have just released a new line of almost-ready-to-fly kits, one of which is a very nice electric-powered sailplane called the ElectroSoar.

The ElectroSoar is a distinctive-looking ship with a straight wing instead of the polyhedral (multiple angles) you usually see in sailplanes. It's built from wood, which will make it much easier to repair if necessary. The electric power system is direct drive, with a very nice scimitar-blade folding prop and spinner.

The slim fuselage of the ElectroSoar doesn't have a lot of room. As a result, the best radio system to use in it is the Futaba MCR-4A. Since this radio doesn't need a separate battery for the receiver, and the receiver and speed control are in one package, it saves a lot of space.

Wing. Assembling the wing consists of simply gluing the two halves together. Be very careful that they are *perfectly* aligned. Any twisting will make the plane very hard to control.

My ElectroSoar had a slight warp in one wing panel. I discovered it after the wings were joined, by laying the wing on my building board so that the root of one wing panel was flat. Then I weighted the

The ElectroSoar is a sleek-looking almost-ready-to-fly Electric job that flies beautifully. It's built of wood, and a motor and folding prop are included in the kit.

wing with sandbags at the center, to be sure the root end would stay flat. Looking at the wingtip showed that the trailing edge of the wing was touching the table, but the leading edge was up about an eighth of an inch. This condition is called *wash-in,* and is not healthy.

It was easy to correct the wing warp by shrinking the covering to hold the wing structure rigid. First I put a spacer under the trailing edge at the wingtip to hold it about a quarter of an inch off the surface of the table. Then I used a sandbag to weight the wingtip down to touch the tabletop. (The root of the wing was still weighted flat.) This made some wrinkles come out in the covering. Using a heat gun, I shrank the covering over the entire upper surface of the wing panel, working from the tip inward. When I removed the spacer

and weight from the wingtip, the trailing edge was warped upward about an eighth of an inch. This condition is called *washout,* and will help the plane fly more smoothly.

I repeated the process with the other wing panel: weighting the center section flat, blocking up the trailing edge of the wingtip, and shrinking the covering on the top of the wing. The result was a wing with the same amount of washout (upward warp at the trailing edge of the wingtip) in each panel.

Fuselage Assembly. The tail surfaces are solid sheet, pre-covered and assembled. When you glue them in, check carefully to make sure that they're straight. I found that the pre-cut slots in the fuselage made this simple.

The motor needs to be all the way down in the

Jeff Troy is about to toss the ElectroSoar for another flight. Launch it straight and level, and it climbs all by itself.

The ElectroSoar comes with a motor, spinner, and folding prop. There's plenty of room for a seven-cell battery pack. The receiver mounts in the space behind the motor.

plastic motor mount to establish the proper thrust line. Make sure it's properly inserted, and hold it in place with a doubled rubber band.

When you tighten the prop nut, don't get it too tight; you can deform the spinner backplate, which will make the whole thing wobble.

I cut out the canopy with scissors, outside the lines molded into it. After several test-fittings and trimmings, I secured it with three screws on either side.

Measure the pushrod lengths against the sides of the fuselage before you cut them.

I finished up the fuselage by putting Velcro patches in the fuselage to hold the main battery pack in place. I shifted it slightly forward to bring the balance point of the plane out where it's shown on the plans.

Flying. The sleek, snappy-looking Electro-Soar flies as good as it looks. The power package has plenty of poop on a seven-cell battery pack to take you up to thermal altitude three or four times. I found that I could establish a good climb, trim in some up elevator to hold it, and just let the plane level off when I eased the power back. Nice!

The ElectroSoar will turn sharply with enough control. After the first few flights, I moved the clevises on the rudder and elevator horns all the way to the innermost holes. This gave me more than enough control throw to do anything I please. I can hang the plane on a wingtip, turning tightly to get back into a thermal. I enjoy soaring flight, and the ElectroSoar's straight wing soars with the best of 'em. It really looks great up there.

WORLD ENGINES BLACK EAGLE

The Black Eagle is a unique ready-built electric plane imported by World Engines and available from them and Indy RC Sales. It's also available in hobby stores that stock the World line.

The most striking thing about the Black Eagle is its pylon-mounted engine. This has a couple of advantages. It's simple to mount and easy to adjust the engine. Cooling is no problem. And there's no chance of bending the engine shaft on a nose-low landing, which happens fairly often on conventional planes.

Another unique feature of the Black Eagle's construction is the tissue-covered flying surfaces! I'm sure this was done for reduced weight, but in practice it works out to be a flaw. The normal wear and tear of storing the plane and transporting it are going to poke holes in the tissue, and there's nothing you can do about it. Since the fuselage, rudder, and elevator have to be covered anyway, my suggestion is to apply a lightweight iron-on covering to the tissue-covered surfaces. You can put the covering right down over the tissue easily enough, or you can cut the tissue panels out with a sharp knife. I used SIG Supercoat film, which is very lightweight and goes on at a low temperature. It's important not to warp the flying surfaces when you're shrinking the film, so use a low temperature and work slowly.

The packaging of the kit is outstanding. All parts are nestled in a Styrofoam box that protects the relatively fragile wing and tail. Instead of a lid, a cardboard sleeve slips over the box.

Assembly. As so often happens with imported models, the instructions need better translation, as the "interesting" English could easily be confusing to a beginner. Fortunately, the illustrations are excellent, and assembly is a simple process.

Overall, construction is outstanding. One mild surprise is that the fuselage, fin, elevator, and rudder aren't covered, and the instructions don't tell you when they should be covered. I covered mine with SIG iron-on Supercoat, but any iron-on film will do nicely.

The fin and rudder need a little bit of shaping; a square of sandpaper is included for the purpose. Round off the leading edge and top of the fin, and sand the top of the rudder so that it blends smoothly with the top of the fin. The leading edge of the rudder should be sanded to a slight point, so the hinges can be inserted a little deeper into the pre-cut slots.

Engine Wiring. The Black Eagle includes a neat little wiring harness for the engine. It has an external switch to allow you to turn the motor on before launch. This setup won't let you turn the motor on and off in the air, but it's perfectly adequate for flying the way it is. You'll have to stay up

The World Engines Black Eagle is a unique ready-built electric model with a pylon-mounted motor. Wings and tail are pre-built and covered with tissue.

until the battery runs down, that's all . . . and you'll only have *one* chance to land!

The instructions suggest that you can set up a third servo to turn the motor switch on and off. It doesn't show you how to attach the pushrod to the switch, however. I made up my own wiring harness, with a servo and a micro switch. The servo is plugged into the throttle channel of the radio, so I can use the throttle lever to turn the engine on and off. My harness uses special super-flexible wire from JoMar; you can also buy wire like this from SR Batteries, Ace RC, and Astro Flight. I made up my wiring harness ahead of time, before building the wing or installing the motor pylon.

The motor servo uses a single output arm. The micro switch is glued to the side of the servo at an angle. When I move the throttle to full, the servo arm swings over and closes the micro switch. It's a simple setup and it has worked well for me.

Wing. The wing is assembled by gluing the outer panels to the center section. If you're going to cover them with an iron-on, do it before attaching the outer panels. The instructions tell you to prop up each tip 11.5 cm. If you fit the root edges flat together, you'll find that the angle you get is half that: The tips are just under 6 cm up. I called World, and they said that the pre-set angle of the parts is correct. I glued the panels on with Slow Jet, which gave me a little time to make certain the panels were straight.

There is a *right* and a *wrong* way to glue the outer wing panels on! Test fit each panel in place before applying any glue. If the outer panel doesn't fit *precisely* with the outer edge of the center section, try the other outer panel.

The motor mount pylon attaches easily to blocks built into the wing center section. Be sure to attach the pylon so that the motor points slightly

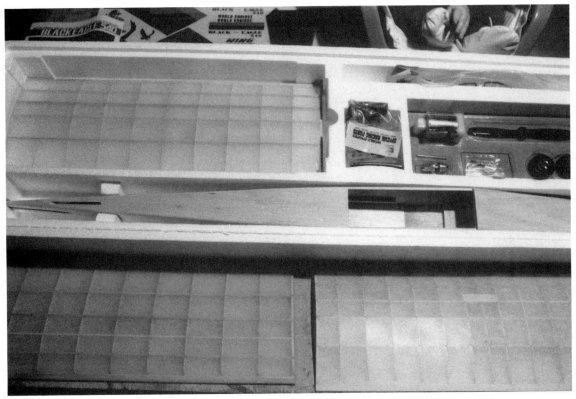

The Black Eagle's parts come protected by a Styrofoam box. Wing and tail sections are pre-covered with tissue; you have to cover the fuselage.

to the right. This offset thrust will help keep your trim from changing when the power comes on in midair.

The motor comes with two capacitors soldered to the terminals to help suppress possible radio interference. I really appreciated having this soldering done at the factory; it's always tough for me to make solder stick to a motor case!

Decoration. Don't try to cut the self-adhesive decals out in big pieces! They'll curl and stick to themselves. Line up the outer edges with the edges of the wing and work inward. Don't try to pull the decal up if it isn't straight!

Radio Installation. Another nice feature of the Black Eagle is the fact that it's set up for standard size servos, so you don't need a radio with anything special. I used the new JR Max system, which is an excellent quality system that is priced low for the sport flier. JR radios have long been favorites of mine. Not only are they very good electronically, but they're full of features that make life easier, such as the complete packages of servo mounting hardware. The Max transmitter is designed to fit the hand comfortably, and the sticks have a good feel. The receiver is small, and the flat battery pack will fasten into the Black Eagle fuselage easily with a piece of double-sided tape. In fact, the fuselage was wide enough for me to put the receiver in right next to the motor control servo.

Measure the pushrods against the side of the fuselage, and bend them so that they will project out of the holes in the rear fuselage. It's easier to get the pushrods installed before you put the servos in, so you can get your fingers into the rear of the radio compartment.

The servo rails glue onto two rails that are already in place in the fuselage. Mark and drill holes for the screws, glue the rails in, and install the ser-

The Black Eagle's motor sits on a pylon on the center of the wing. It's hard to break the prop when you land! The prop and spinner are included in the kit.

vos . . . it doesn't get any easier than this.

I used Du-Bro pushrod connectors to attach the rods to the servo arms, rather than making Z-bends in the rods. This gives me more room to make adjustments.

At this point, you're ready to charge up and go flying. It only took me two brief evenings to have the Black Eagle ready to go. Nice engineering!

Flying. The battery compartment is just big enough to get a six-cell sub-C pack in it, which is too bad; I like to use seven-cell 800 MAh packs, too. Seven cells would give the Black Eagle a faster climb—not that it really *needs* it.

One thing I discovered immediately was that the Black Eagle is noisier than most electric models! The engine pylon vibrates slightly, and this causes a drumming effect on the wing covering. It's not an annoying noise, but you certainly don't have

any problem telling whether or not your engine is still running!

I picked a spring evening when the winds were dead calm for my first flights. In these conditions, the Eagle did beautifully. I could get up to a good altitude with a three-minute motor run. If there were any thermals around, I didn't find them, so I made two climbs and descents and set up for landing. There was more than enough power for a missed approach and a go-around.

The next flying session was on my lunch hour the next day. Winds were gusting up to 5 mph, and there was bright sunshine. The Eagle showed a tendency to get blown around, especially when I was careless enough to let the wing get under a wingtip; I had to put the nose down and apply full opposite rudder a couple of times. Once I figured out how to keep my turns flat, I made it up to a

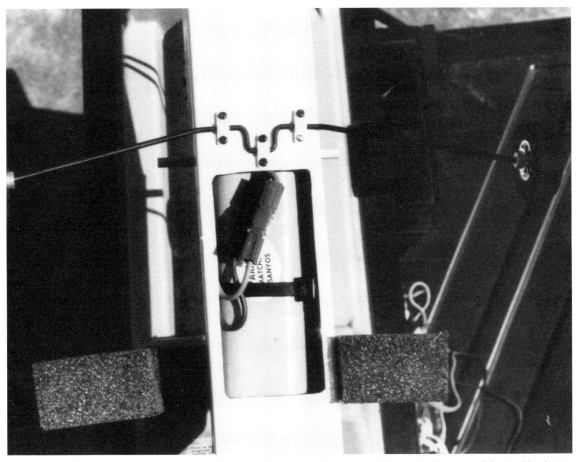

The Black Eagle has a compartment in the underside of the nose section for the battery pack. It's too small for anything larger than a six-cell pack.

decent altitude and shut off the engine.

A little mooching around got me into a pretty good thermal. I kept my turns flat, and left it to turn upwind after a few minutes. Like many light airplanes, the Eagle needs speed to penetrate into the wind, and I didn't want to fight my way back to the field. I found that I could make long, slow figure-eights into the wind and maintain altitude nicely. I brought the Eagle in after a very satisfying 10-minute flight. Thanks to some nearby trees, the air was turbulent near the ground, and I had to wrestle it in with the motor running. That's another nice feature of a pylon-mounted engine: It makes power-on landings much easier!

All in all, the Black Eagle is a very good little trainer plane. Kit engineering and quality are excellent, although I think the tissue covering for the wings is a poor choice. It's a gentle flier in calm conditions that will give you many satisfying flights.

A

Radio Control Manufacturers, Suppliers, and Organizations

Academy of Model Aeronautics
1810 Samuel Morse Drive
Reston, VA 22090
The national organization for model fliers.

Ace RC
116 West 19th St.
Higginsville, MO 64037
Electronic kits, model kits, famous Silver Seven radios, Four Stroke Squadron.

Airtronics, Inc.
11 Autry
Irvine, CA 92718-2709
RC systems, kits.

Ambrosia Microcomputer Products
15 W 721 82nd St.
Hinsdale, IL 60521
"RC Aerochopper" flight simulator for Atari computers.

Applied Design Corporation
738 Penn Street
El Segundo, CA 90245
Sanding and finishing products.

Art Gross Enterprises
12516 Maplewood Ave.
Edmonds, WA 98020
Wedge Lock sanding tools.

Astro Flight
13311 Beach Ave.
Venice, CA 90291
Electric flight systems, kits.

Beemer RC West Distributors, Inc.
7725 E Redfield Dr. Suite 105
Scottsdale, AZ 85260
Multiplex RC systems, sales and service.

C/B Tatone Products Corp.
21658 Cloud Way
Hayward, CA 94545
Engine mounts, mufflers, accessories, test stands.

Cannon RC Systems
2828 Cochran St. Suite 281
Simi Valley, CA 93065
Lightweight miniature RC systems.

Carl Goldberg Models
4732 W. Chicago Ave.
Chicago, IL 60651
Trainer planes, scale kits, jet adhesives, accessories.

Charlie's R/C Goodies
2828 Cochran St. Suite 281
Simi Valley, CA 93065
G-mark engines, electric flight supplies.

Compuserve
5000 Arlington Centre Blvd.
Columbus, OH 43220
Personal computer network, includes ModelNet.

Coverite
420 Babylon Road
Horsham, PA 19044
Covering materials, kits, accessories.

Cox Hobbies
1525 E. Warner
Santa Ana, CA 92705
.049 engines, kits, RC systems, ready-to-fly planes.

Custom Electronics
8870 Hamilton St.
Alta Loma, CA 91701
Electronic devices for transmitters, receivers, and servos.

Custom Racing Products
3250 El Camino Real B3
Atascadero, CA 93422
Chargers, battery cyclers, RC car kits.

Dave Brown Products
4560 Layhigh Road
Hamilton, OH 45013
Accessories, wheels, RC Flight Simulator for personal computers.

Davey Systems Corp.
675 Tower Lane
West Chester, PA 19380
Sailplane kits, electric power kits, winches, electric motors, accessories.

Doug's Hobby Shop
Rt. 301 Box 96 C
Waldorf, MD 20601
Mail order hobby supplies, electric experts.

Du-Bro Products
480 Bonner Road
Wauconda, IL 60084
Accessories, tools, wheels, hardware.

Dynaflite, Inc.
1578 Osage
San Marcos, CA 92065
Fun scale kits, sailplane kits, accessories.

Electronic Model Systems
2248 Mission Hills Lane
Yorba Linda, CA 92686
Batteries, electronic supplies.

Fiberglass Master
Route 1 Box 350
Goodview, VA 24095
Fiberglass cowls and wheel pants for popular kits.

Flyline Models
10643 Ashby Place
Fairfax, VA 22030
Schoolyard Scale kits.

Futaba
4 Studebaker
Irvine, CA 92718
RC systems, accessories.

Great Planes Manufacturing
706 West Bradley
Urbana, IL 61801
Model kits, accessories.

Grish Brothers
P. O. Box 248
St. John, IN 46373
Propellers, accessories.

H & N Electronics
10937 Rome Beauty Drive
California City, CA 93505
Electronic accessories, Supersafe solder flux.

Hannan's Runway
Box A
Escondido, CA 92025
Books and model supplies.

Hobby Dynamics
P. O. Box 3276
Champaign, IL 61821
JR radios, kits, engines.

Hobby Horn
15173 Moran Street
Westminster, CA 92683
Old Timer kits, electric kits and flight systems.

Hobby Lobby International
Route 3 Franklin Pike Cir.
Brentwood, TN 37027
Graupner kits, accessories, tools, large catalog.

Hobby Shack
18480 Bandilier Circle
Fountain Valley, CA 92708
Kits, ready-to-fly planes, RC systems, engines, accessories; large catalog.

Indy RC
10620 N. College Ave.
Indianapolis, IN 46280
Kits, engines, ready-to-fly planes, large catalog.

J&Z Products
25029 South Vermont Avenue
Harbor City, CA 90710
Props, spinners, accessories.

J'Tec
164 School St.
Daly City, CA 94014
Engine mounts, hardware, in-cowl mufflers, accessories.

Jomar
2028 Knightsbridge
Cincinnati, OH 45244
Electric motor speed controllers, engine sync systems, accessories.

Kraft Midwest
117 E. Main St.
Northville, MI 48167
RC system repair and tuning, Kraft radio parts.

Larry Jolly Models
5501 West Como
Santa Ana, CA 92703
Sailplane and electric flight model kits.

Leisure Electronics
22971 B Triton Way
Laguna Hills, CA 92653
Electric flight systems, chargers, Old Timer kits.

MRC
200 Carter Dr.
Edison, NJ 08817
Ready-to-fly airplanes, RC systems, radios, engines, model rockets, RC cars.

Midwest Products
400 South Indiana
Hobart, IN 46342
Kits, accessories, wood and building supplies.

Novak Electronics
128 E. Dyer Rd. #c
Santa Ana, CA 92707
Chargers, speed controllers, electronic accessories.

PIC Penn International Chemicals
3 Old Trail
Ormond Beach, FL 32074
Adhesives, chemical products.

Parma International
13927 Progress Parkway
N. Royalton, OH 44133
Electric kits, RC cars, accessories.

Paul K. Guillow, Inc.
40 New Salem St.
Wakefield, MA 01880
Scale model kits.

Peck-Polymers
9962 Prospect Suite L
Santee, CA 92071
Kits, supplies, RC Blimp kit, CO2 motors.

Polk's Hobbies
346 Bergen Ave.
Jersey City, NJ 07304
Kits, engines, RC systems, accessories, tools.

Product Design Inc.
16922 N E 124th St.
Redmond, WA 98052
Speed controllers.

RAM
4734 N. Milwaukee Ave.
Chicago, IL 60630
Electric accessories, speed controllers, boat kits.

Robart
310 North 5th
St. Charles, IL 60714
Tools, accessories, speed controllers.

Robbe Model Sport
180 Township Line Road
Bellemead, NJ 08502
Kits, almost-ready-to-fly airplanes, chargers, accessories.

Royal Electronics
2380 S. Holly Pl
Denver, CO 80222
Receiver kits, servo kits, batteries and accessories.

Royal Products Corporation
790 West Tennessee Ave.
Denver, CO 80223
Kits, ready-to-fly models, engines, accessories.

SR Batteries
P. O. Box 287
Belleport, NY 11713
High-performance batteries for RC systems, electric flight.

Satellite City
P. O. Box 836
Simi, CA 93062-0836
Hot Stuff CyA adhesives, accessories.

Sermos RC Connectors
28 Jay Road
Stamford, CT 06905
Connectors

Sheldon's Hobby Shop
2135 Old Oakland Rd.
San Jose, CA 95131
Mail-order kits and supplies.

SIG Manufacturing
401 S. Front St.
Montezuma, IA 50171
Kits, engines, RC systems, paint and covering, accessories, large catalog.

Sonic-Tronics
7865 Mill Road
Elkins Park, PA 19117
Accessories, glow plugs, fuel pumps, folding props.

Sullivan Products
1 N. Haven St.
Baltimore, MD 21224
Accessories, starters, pushrods, tanks, hardware.

TRC Engineering
0-10972 10th Ave. NW
Grand Rapids, MI 49504
Impulse II and Impulse IV fast chargers.

Top Flite Models
2801 S. 25th Ave.
Broadview, IL 60153-4589
MonoKote covering, scale and sailplane kits, trainers, props.

Tower Hobbies
1608 Interstate Dr.
Champaign, IL 61821
Kits, engines, radio systems, Kyosho ARF kits, large catalog.

United Model Distributors
301 Holbrook Dr.
Wheeling, IL 60090
Engines, ready-to-fly planes.

Victor Engineering
19572 Waterburg Lane
Huntington Beach, CA 92646
Chargers, accessories.

Williams Brothers, Inc.
181 Pawnee St.
San Marcos, CA 92069
Parts and accessories for scale models, plastic kits, pilot figures.

Windsor Propeller Company
384 Tesconi Court
Santa Rosa, CA 95401
Master Airscrew props and accessories.

World Engines
8960 Rossash Ave.
Cincinnati, OH 45236
Engines, radio systems, ready-to-fly kits, accessories.

B

Magazines, Publishers, and Booksellers

Flying Models Magazine
Box 700
Newton, NJ 07860

Kalmbach Publishing
21027 Crossroads Circle
Waukesha, WI 53187

Model Airplane News
632 Danbury Road
Georgetown, CT 06829

Model Aviation Magazine
1810 Samuel Morse Drive
Reston, VA 22090

Model Builder Magazine
898 W. 16th St.
Newport Beach, CA 92663-2802

Motorbooks International
729 Prospect Ave.
Osceola, WI 54020

RC Report
P. O. Box 1706
Huntsville, AL 35807

RC Soaring Digest
P. O. Box 1079
Payson, AZ 85547

RC Video Magazine
1200 Diamond Circle Unit J
Lafayette, CO 80026

Radio Control Modeler Magazine
144 W. Sierra Madre Blvd.
Sierra Madre, CA 91024

Scale RC Modeler
7950 Deering Ave.
Canoga Park, CA 91304

Squadron/Signal Publications
1115 Crowley Drive
Carrollton, TX 75006

TAB Books
Blue Ridge Summit, PA 17294-0850

Zenith Aviation Books
P. O. Box 1
Osceola, WI 54020

Index

Index